I am dedicating this book to the four people who have inspired me the most. They, without doubt, are my sons Cody, Cameron, Carson, and Carter. Without their love and support this book would not have been possible. Many times I gave up the keyboard and thought that I did not need to finish, but then one of my sons would ask about it and want to read it. Time after time I wanted to give up, but time after time they unknowingly pushed me back to complete the goal I set twelve years ago. Thank you boys for being the driving force that kept me focused during the writing of this book and thank you for doing your part today to be as happy and productive as you are now.

I love you guys

-Dad

The Different One

A story of a kid and his journey to manhood

By Bobby Howell

My Life

Sitting there under the bridge in my work van, I became entranced by the sounds of the cars as they sped overhead. One by one the dull clicking sound from the tires transferring from road to bridge put me in a rhythm that kick-started my thinking. I began to replay the events in my life and they came in vivid color. They started when I was young and played out as if I were watching a movie. Scene after scene I could feel the emotions of the moments as each memory came into focus. Little things like the time I accidentally put the car in neutral and it rolled down the hill into a cow pasture. Then there was the time I ran through fresh poured concrete and tried to hide the fact it was me.

Bad memories came flooding back as well. These memories hit me hard and as I thought of them that dry, painful lump formed in my throat. I began to question myself; why did I make it and how come I was different from other people that have lived through similar situations? As a result of all this thinking I began to remember things that I thought I had put out of my mind. Some things never go away and this was never more evident than right now. I sat in that van and I could not clear my mind of the events that changed my life.

 My mothers' death, my father going to prison and being homeless all came back. Those emotions were felt even more. I reflected in the heat for almost two hours going over all the good and bad times I had while growing up and I began to realize that I was kind of unique.

I had gained a lot of life experience and I would be doing a huge injustice if I did not share what I had experienced. I was not a professional football player like I had hoped to be. I was not a movie star or politician or a rock star. I was a common man trying to live the American dream.

At the time I had a wife and two kids, a great job and a place to call home. There was nothing that set me apart from the rest of the world. Somehow I began to feel inspired to write down what it was I lived through and share it. I had so many things I wanted to share and I knew if I did, I could change the way a kid thought about their situation. I wanted more than anything to give hope to a child like it was given to me. In an instant I felt a huge responsibility come over me and I knew then that people needed to hear what I had to say.

I picked up my yellow legal pad and started from the beginning. Once my pen hit the paper I was in the zone. It was easy to tell my story. The pages of the pad began to fill up and I could no longer hear the cars nor did I even notice the afternoon Arizona sun. My surroundings seemed to slow to a crawl and then to a stop. There were no sounds or movements that distracted from my mission.

As I wrote my way through my life, I started to realize that I was subjected to some very challenging things at a very young age. I was asked to do things that nobody, much less a kid should do. As a young father it dawned on me that I have a gift. My desire to share my experience to help others grew to an overwhelming level. My excitement expanded as I drifted deeper into my life story.

I was on fire and nothing was going to stop me! That was until a knock came on my window. Looking up a glare caught my eye. It was a Phoenix Police Officer and that glare was the afternoon sun bouncing off his badge. He inquired about what it was I was doing and I could tell he was somewhat puzzled. I told him I was writing my life story. He looked around for a quick minute just to make sure he heard me right and to make sure of our location. Even more confused he asked, "Do you realize you are under a bridge"? I knew where he was going so I replied, "yes," and told him I would only be a few more minutes and then I would be on my way. I raised my pad of paper and gave him a polite smile in hopes that might satisfy him. Again he looked around to just to verify our location and my motive. "You have been parked here six hours," he calmly replied. Six hours! I looked at my watch and he was right. I had taken my lunch break at eleven and it was five o'clock. I was completely taken off guard. I began to panic. I had wasted a whole day of work and now I was going to be late coming home. The officer was kind enough to push me on my way without any trouble. After all, I was sitting in a neighborhood known for drug sales for six hours in a van. He had every right to be suspicious of me.

I had about an hour drive home and I was stuck thinking about all the things I had just written in my legal pad. I had become completely consumed with what I had started. The stories kept flowing as I was stuck in the afternoon rush hour traffic of Phoenix. Unable to get on with my writing my mind was on fire with the prospect of how this whole thing would turn out. Then as quickly as I got excited I began to question myself. Was I being silly to think that the things I lived through were good enough to inspire today's youth? Was I being self-absorbed and pounding my chest a little too much? I began to doubt myself and discredit all the work I had just put in.

As if I had planned it for dramatic effect, my mind was enlightened and the answer came to me. I was a common man that lived an uncommon childhood. I didn't need to be a movie star or professional football player to validate my past; I was my own hero and being common was ok with me. I rose from the dumps and dregs of the earth and now I was living a life of happiness and fulfillment. My childhood sucked and I had every excuse to fail and be mediocre. I was able to succeed when many had written me off as a statistic.

This is when I truly knew my story could help. Everyone has a checkered past and we all have our own story to share. I know my story will touch many and it is my goal that you too can find the joy, happiness, and love I have found. No matter where we come from, we all have the ability to direct our destiny and it is my hope that my life will bless yours.

The Beginning

I know by writing this story that I will bring up bad feelings and stir up bad memories for some of those that are close to me. I have made the choice to take that chance, because I feel that what I have to say will help others in my same position. I hope it will help those who were involved in my childhood to talk about and resolve their feelings. What I am about to tell you is told through my eyes only. I am sure that the other people involved would dispute or confirm in more detail if we had them tell their story. It is important for me to tell it like I saw it. I feel that the way we see things shapes who we become.

This story is only intended for those who are looking for answers as to why as young children we are sometimes forced into a life of trials and hardships. Too many times in my life I have seen children damaged by parents or other adults in a leadership role who has their own unresolved past. This creates a cycle that if not changed, will continue to snowball and effect many generations.

It is my hope that what I say will inspire my siblings and others to share their stories. The kids in my family are special and we have a story that needs to be shared with others. What children go through in their childhood is not their fault. We try to follow the examples set for us but if those examples are sub-par, what are we to do? The answer is simple. When we find ourselves in that same position, we do our best to be the example we never got.

It is up to the exploited, misguided and neglected youth of today to be the positive leaders of tomorrow. For some, it is easy to blame others and take the easy road out when things get tough. I know without a shadow of a doubt that if we can find the strength to carry on we will prevail and change the cycle we were once a part of.

Growing up like my siblings and I did is a testament to the desire and human spirit that we all possess. As an adult I know that children are resilient and able to withstand the trials and tribulations that befall us all. Remembering all the events of my life made me sit and wonder why I did not see the severity of what was happening. Why did we make it and how was it possible? These are questions I have asked myself for many years. I didn't come to a conclusion until I was about halfway through this book.

What I came up with was that life has a way of conditioning us to achieve the plan set forth for us as adults. For me it was the birth of my four sons that really drove that fact home. When they came, I knew exactly what to do and had the drive and determination to follow through. I made the decision at the age of fourteen that I would be nothing like my father when I had kids. My actions were instant when I discovered I was a soon to be father.

Ultimately, we make the choice of how we deal with the trials of life, but I am now a firm believer that what we were exposed to as children influences those choices we make as adults. I am not saying that we should use this knowledge or understanding as an excuse to dismiss our actions. In my own personal life I have not always made the right choices as it pertains to health, wealth and relationships. However, as a father of four successful sons, I feel I have been more than right in the choices I have made on their behalves.

You see, what I am about to tell you is the story of my life and the events that took place that helped mold the father that I am today. I know I have my downfalls and will not always succeed in my endeavors in life, but I also know without a shadow of doubt I will succeed as a father. I was taught at an early age about wrong decisions to make in life and this helped me on my journey to fatherhood.

As you read this story, keep in mind that we all make mistakes and do things we regret. That is not the important part and not the focus of this story. I don't want to pretend that I have the answers to all of life's questions or even act as though I am a wise person. I have just learned that we can be products of our environment and this can affect the choices we make in life. What you do with those choices and how you choose to deal with the outcome is what is important. A friend once told me "It doesn't matter what you have done or where you have been that matters, it's what you're doing and where you're going that matters". This quote has meant the world to me. It reminds me that I can always refocus my life and choose another path. It is my hope that my story might touch you in a way that you might refocus your life and change if need be. I am not a doctor or a person of extreme wisdom. I am just a common man who lived through an uncommon life. So this is it, hope you enjoy.

Prescott

I was born is a small town named Prescott, Arizona in 1975. This is the kind of town you see on a postcard. There is an old courthouse that stands in the middle of the town square surrounded by historic buildings on all sides. The trees are big and the breeze sends the sweet smell of spring through the air. The snow in the winter piles high and provides a playland equal to no other. This is a picture perfect town with beautiful sights and sounds. From the small town parades to the art shows to the rodeo, I can still smell the cotton candy and see the balloons. This is the place where every kid wants to live.

I was the youngest of four children. There was Laurie, my oldest sister, who had a different father than I. Then there was Doug, my brother, who also had a different father than I. Next was Tammy. She is my only "full-blooded" sibling. Lastly there was me. I point out the difference in fathers, as it will play a major role in this story. Even though we kids loved each other there was always a feeling of separation from having different fathers. I am a firm believer that my father used this fact as a weapon and as an excuse to justify his behaviors. I don't want to jump ahead so let's refocus.

We were not wealthy by any means. We lived in a run down, almost shanty type house behind a liquor store. When the snows came we would build snow forts and tunnels in the field behind the liquor store. The interior walls were made of multiple layers of cardboard. This store is one of my earliest memories because it had a huge barrel as its sign. It's funny what we remember. Even today when I drive by that sign it stirs up memories from my early years. The house is long gone but that sign stands strong almost as marker of my existence. Every time I visit Prescott I drive by the store and smile to myself. I have caught myself saying, "That's me!" under my breath.

Times were good when I was little. Of course I was a very young child and so I think it was natural for things to be good. I now know that the truth is a little darker than what I remember. Listening to the stories as an adult, it is easy to see that life was bleak right from the start.

My father is what you would call a hot head. He had a very short fuse and a huge temper to follow. My father could make people obey and conform just by raising his voice. He is not big in stature but he could intimidate the biggest of men. There was a look in his eye that let people know he was serious when he spoke. He was intense and there was no doubt when he was mad. I know that everyone at some point in their lives thinks that their father was mean but I think there was a touch of evil in mine.

Violence was a large part of my childhood. Mostly due to the example my father set for me. I don't remember any violence outside the house. It was always in the house, behind closed doors where no one could see. I remember one time Doug was thrown through a wall at this shanty house that we lived in. I don't know why, but I'm sure it was a petty offense at best. There are not a lot of memories of Prescott as I was too young. I do, however, know that there was a lot of hatred between my mother's family and my father's. I would later hear stories of fights and plans of sabotage between my uncles and father. I will tell you that I was not aware of this for some time.

Many times I have tried to get answers as to what really happened. In typical dysfunctional fashion, all the adults involved digressed into name calling and finger-pointing. Honestly, I just got tired of it and quit asking. I know there was plenty of animosity and ill feelings between all parties. This was my father's style and there is no doubt in my mind the there was substantial violence taking place. Both adults and children have felt the evil my father possesses.

For whatever reason I was spared the wrath of my father and never subject to his anger or physical lashings out, maybe because he knew I would be the last or he felt a special bond with me. Whatever the reason, I was treated differently from the rest. Again this is another question that will go unanswered.

When I was born, my father got a tattoo of a baby devil on his left forearm that read "Bob's Little Devil". I guess in his eyes I was the chosen one. By all accounts I was the last of his bloodline and he wanted me to carry it on. There is a rumor of him having another son in St. Louis but that has never been confirmed. I guess I will never know why I was spared but there have been times that I wish it had been me receiving his wrath. I wanted so much to not be singled out. I didn't want my brother and sisters to hate me because I was the one that sat on the sidelines and watched.

As you will later read, there was a lot of violence and pain inflicted by my father on my siblings. There is still not a day that goes by that I don't wish I could have stood in their place and felt what they had to feel. I can't say what it was like to be in their shoes but I can tell you how it feels to have your heart ripped out and the extreme pain I felt when I watched it happen to others. There is still that pain in the pit of my stomach when I talk about it.

The pain that was inflicted on me was not physical. It was mental. Many times I have been trapped with my own thoughts and he has taken a toll on me. The most painful part of the mind games came when my father would, at my young age, turn me against those that I loved in order to protect him. I was used as a pawn in his sick chess game. He felt if he could use me to keep the others in check, then he would have free reign to do as he pleased. Many times in my young life, my father would tell my sister that I would hate her and that I would be taken away if she told of his exploits. This kind of terrorism is very effective and damaging to a kid who is six to ten years of age. With his plan in place and rule-with-fist attitude, there was nothing we kids could do to stop the sick intentions of this man.

The Run Away

I think living in Prescott got to be too much for my father. He must have run out of friends and felt like he needed to run away. As a result of a fight with my mother, he decided to take me and go to Hamilton, Ohio where his mother lived. He took me because he knew he had control of the situation as long as I remained his little pawn. I was very young; maybe four, and my father knew that my mother would do anything to get me back.

I remember this was the first time I flew on an airplane and he made me feel like I was special. It was a big TWA plane and I vividly remember walking off the plane in Ohio thinking I was the king. I was taught to take care of him and stand ready to defend him if necessary. I'm not talking defend in a physical way. There is so much power when a four-year-old kid cries and runs to his father in times of distress. I had become his insurance policy and he was playing it for all it was worth.

The smell of the jet fuel stung my nose when the hatch on the plane opened. There we were in a strange place without my family. I was confused and excited. I was a young kid and didn't understand a lot, so I just followed my father's lead and went with what he said. I vaguely recall asking my father why we left and he told me, "I am a good guy and people don't like me because I am nice." I would hear this many times during my childhood. I think he knew a time would come that he would need an ally and he wanted it to be me. It was working because I thought my father was a god and whatever said he was the gospel. I stood up for my father so many times in my life that when I finally knew the truth I was devastated and ashamed of what I had done. There were times I had completely turned my back on my loved ones to stand up for my father. At the age of fifteen I saw the web he had spun and the truth set me free.

We were only in Ohio for a short time but while there my father put in some serious work on me. I was being trained to be his little warrior. Day after day he would treat me to things I know my brother and sisters never had. There is one picture I have that tells all. It is a picture of the two of us at an air show in Hamilton. We were pals and he was creating this life so when needed, I could bail him out. But as he had done many times before, he burned his bridge or owed someone money so he decided that we should return to be with the rest of the family.

The separation from my family must have been traumatic enough event to alert my consciousness because this is when I begin to really remember the happenings of my life. This is when the dark cloud floated overhead and one by one the things I saw began to form my life.

I was sitting on the porch of my grandmother's house when my father began to prep me for my return trip. It went something like this: "Your mother can't survive without me so we need to go back". I was excited because I missed my family. Then he told me, "Your damn brother and sisters are causing problems for your mom." I wondered why but my only option was to take his word and follow his directions.

With that we were headed back to be with the family. I didn't want to go because I was his little buddy and I didn't want to share him with the others. I wanted the ice cream and the airplane shows all to myself. His plan was working. I didn't want my family. I wanted only him. Slowly, he was conditioning me to not be his son but to be his follower. Much like a cult leader trains his flock I was becoming a manipulated clone to have at his disposal. That was the first time I remember saying, "I love you daddy".

San Diego

My mother decided that the rest of my family should leave Prescott and move to San Diego. I'm not sure why they moved but I'm sure it had to do with my mother's health, or maybe she just wanted a fresh start. Soon after they moved, my father and I returned to live with the rest of the family in San Diego. From what I can remember we were still living in poverty without much promise of that changing. We lived in a rundown house in the rough part of town. We kids were always dirty and we didn't live in the best of conditions. Still to this day I can smell that sour damp smell that infested the whole house. It was common to see roaches scamper through the house when the lights were turned on.

The old kitchen floor was so dirty that it would turn your feet black when you walked on it barefoot. Dirty laundry filled the house, and with the addition of a dog named "Rusty", that house was a disaster. If the house was in that shape I can assure you that our personal hygiene was lacking. It was a step up from the cardboard shanty house but it still was far from desirable conditions.

I am not sure if my father was working but I know that we were always on welfare as long as I could remember. Food was scarce and it was a constant cycle of the water or the electric being turned off. Never did we feel completely comfortable in that house. No matter how hungry we were, there was always beer and cigarettes in the house. Somehow I kept the faith and stuck up for my father.

Not all times were bad. My brother and I were slowly becoming best of buddies without my father knowing. He was my big bro and I remember wanting to be like him. He was funny and it was the early eighties and he had the curly hair everyone wanted. This included me. I wanted so bad to be like him. No matter how bad it got I could always rely on him to put a smile on my face.

I recall one time when my father took us fishing in the harbor. It was a great time for me, and a memory that has lasted the test of time. I went with my brother and he had a way of making me feel like a champ. There we the two of us standing on the pier hoping to hook a big one. The smell of the ocean and fish filled my nasal passages and the breeze was slight and had a chill to it. There we were, just the two of us sitting on the end of the pier without a care or worry.

While reeling in his line something hit his line hard. We both shot to our feet and bounced around like a couple kids who sat on an ant pile. The faster he would reel in the line the more the fishing rod bent. I remember shouting, "You caught the big one" over and over. Just as quick as we got excited, we were deflated. He caught a coffee can with the lid peeled half way open. When he went to take it off the hook an octopus arm came shooting out. It scared the crap out of us and we both fell back on the pier rolling in laughter. We had a laugh that lasted my whole life. Many times I have revisited that story when I was feeling down and out. Every time it did the trick and brought me back to a place where I could smile again.

Writing this story I see how instrumental my brother was in the safety and success of my life. He made the decision at a young age to set aside his own safety to ensure mine. As an adult, I see he was protecting me at the expense of himself. My brother shielded me from my father and I now know it was him as well as my sisters that all kept me safe from my father. If it meant taking a beating or a ritualistic punishment he was there to take it. Just as long as I was spared they stood up and took it. Whether it was acting like a clown on the pier to make me laugh or enduring physical pain, my brother was there to accept the call.

It is at this point in my life that I begin to see and hear things that a five-year-old boy should not be exposed to. Let me preface this section by stating that my mother is a saint and should be given all the credit in the world for her efforts in raising her kids. She did the best she could with what she had. Her job as a mother was not an easy one but one she did very well. Due to her health it was hard for her to keep constant tabs on us kids but she did her best. For all intents and purposes she was a single parent and there were four of us. It is understandable that she couldn't be everywhere all the time.

With my father in and out of jail and drunk at home, the responsibility fell on the older kids to help raise and nurture me. Many times my older sister Laurie was left to be the mom. Doug was becoming a father figure to me and I looked up to him. By nature I wanted to be close to him so I followed him most places he went. With my father gone most of the time, I was able to see my brother and sister not for what he tried to have me believe but for the scared kids they were. We all lived in fear and together we somehow weathered the storm.

We actually lived in a suburb of San Diego named Lemon Grove. This was a poor area filled with crime and violence. All the houses looked like ours, old and run down. There were no manicured lawns or swimming pools. There were just dirty kids playing in the dirty streets in front of their dirty houses.

My first real exposure to violence came when my brother and I were walking to the corner store. There was a storage facility at the end of the street where we lived. We would walk by this storage place almost every day and wave to the old man who ran the facility. On this particular day things would change. It was a typical day on our block. The sun was shining and the kids were all in the streets playing. There was nothing to warn us of the events in which we were about to partake.

As we were walking to the store we noticed that something was not quite right. It was kind of like things were slowing down as we approached the storage building. As we got closer the door flew open and the old man charged out yelling for help. He was covered from head to toe with blood. The look of terror on his face is forever etched in my mind. To this point in my life I had never been so scared.

Apparently he was getting robbed and began to put up a fight. During the struggle he was hit in the face and then shot in the face with a flare gun. That's right, I said a flare gun. The blood was gushing from his forehead and flowing down the front of his jacket. What the heck was going on? I began to panic and cry. I was scared and what could I do but follow as my brother ran to get help. After seeing the old man covered in blood and being so scared, I'm not really sure where we ran to for help. For days, I refused to walk by that storage facility. I never saw that old man again. I never got a real answer as to what happened to the old man but I like to believe he just retired and went on to live out his days on a boat somewhere.

I think at that moment I learned the world could be a bad place. That is a hard lesson to learn as a young child. This image has stuck with me for all this time and it still stands as a defining moment in my life. It taught me that everyone can be a victim, even the old man at the end of the street.

While we lived in Lemon Grove we saw a lot of crime and unlawful activity as children. There were many drugs and drug related crimes. It was commonplace, and most of the time no one really paid any attention to what was going on.

One night, as the family was winding down and getting ready for bed we were startled by the roar of motorcycle engines. Not one or two but thirty or forty. They raced up and down the street before they came to rest at a house toward the end of the street. It seems that there was a motorcycle gang that had come to party at a member's house and get rowdy. In typical fashion the booze and drugs began to flow. The music was turned up loud and the party spilled out into the street. My father was out of the house and it was just my mother and us kids.

Actually, I think my father was in the county lock up. I remember two days later we were waiting outside the county lock up waiting for my father to walk up the ramp as he was being released from jail.

Well as the night progressed and the partying got harder, a rival gang decided to crash the party. They rode in on their bikes racing up and down the street yelling and taunting the other gang. Right on cue, as if it were preplanned, a gunshot rang out in the darkness. This erupted into an all out war between the two gangs. It was as if a volcano exploded when they confronted each other. Soon the fight spread to the neighborhood and took us all hostage. The music stopped and the breaking of bottles was silenced.

My Mother ordered us all to the floor as there were guns being fired and men running through the streets looking for strategic places to hide. My sister and I lay on the floor covered by a mattress waiting for the 'all clear' from our mother. We had moved a couple houses down the street but the floor had that sour smell and it was extremely uncomfortable. We lay on that floor for some time just listening and waiting. We could hear a man crawling beneath us in the crawl space of the house. If you have ever lived in a house with a crawl space you know that all that separates you from the crawl space is a wood floor. Six to eight inches from us was a man looking to kill somebody. A faint smell of dust came up through the floorboards. That is how close this guy was. He was kicking up dust from crawling on the ground.

The fight went on for a long time that night. There were so many bikers involved that the police would not come right away. They waited for things to settle a bit before the mounted an offense to arrest and stop the bikers. It was early in the morning before we were allowed to come up from the floor. When we finally got to go to bed I laid there shaking for hours before I could fall asleep. Six years old and I had just been involved in an all out gunfight between two motorcycle gangs.

The thing is that my father was not there to take care of his family. I could never imagine not being there for my family in such a time of need. This kind of thing happened frequently on our street. If it wasn't bikers shooting, it was a husband beating up his wife, or neighbors fighting, or even an old man getting shot in the face.

Evil Happenings

I would like to say that the violence all happened outside the house but I would be lying. My father was a very abusive man and imposed his will on whoever he wanted to. He did not care if you were friend or foe. He was physical not only to his kids but also my mother. He was even abusive to our dogs. His behavior would best be described as explosive and unpredictable. Although I could never confirm it later in life it is my opinion that my father was abused as a child and carried this over to adulthood. There are stories that he was beat and locked in the basement of his house as a means of punishment. It was easy to see that he was carrying on the cycle that was passed on to him. This is the sole motivation that caused me to decide to do whatever it takes to break that cycle and not pass it on to my kids. No matter what happened to me as a kid, I could not let that be an excuse to act like my father did,

This is now a good time to share with you the couple of years that I consider the most detrimental to my childhood. While living In Lemon Grove my mother was battling breast cancer and she truly was in the fight for her life. Looking back now as an adult it amazing to me the strength and love that my mother showed to us. I know without a shadow of a doubt that my mother loved and did her best for her kids till the day she passed and left this earth. It took me a long time to get over the pain and shock of that day. Throughout my life I have often wondered why I lost my mother and why I could not have a normal life. I wanted to live in a world where I could have returned home from school to do homework, play and have dinner with my family. As fate would have it my life did not turn out that way.

There is a lot of grey area surrounding the cancer and treatments of my mother. I have letters that she wrote where she would talk about how she is getting better and seems to be beating the cancer. If this was true I can't help but think about what a waste of a beautiful life. I do however; I believe that things happen for a reason.

I feel in my heart that my mother's death served a purpose. It would seem that she gave the ultimate sacrifice to save her kids. The death of my mother shined the spotlight on my father and exposed a lot of his secrets. This allowed us kids to escape his ill will and allowed us the opportunity to grow and not become a statistic.

I refuse to believe that my mother did not fight to the end. It is her strong will and determination that helps give me the motivation to carry on. No matter how sick she was or how weak, there she was putting her best effort forward. I truly believe that this was the contributing factor to her making a recovery and turning the tables on cancer. Even now at my age her example is deeply rooted in my soul and I continue to carry it with me to this day. Many times I have reflected back and somehow found the strength and courage to push on. I know it's because of my mother and the example she set for her kids. I really only have two memories of my mother. One is her fight with cancer, and the other is her death. I choose to remember her courageous fight and unwavering tenacity.

In one of the letters she talked about all the Christmas presents that we had and that she was feeling so much better. She talked about getting stronger and how her spirits were rising. All signs pointed to her getting better and feeling stronger. This was late in 1981 to early 1982; the science of cancer was not what it is today. For her to be beating this cancer would be nothing short of a miracle. Judging from the letters I hold, she should have made a full recovery. I guess I can speculate as to what should have happened but the fact remains the same. I woke up to find that my mother had passed on and now it was up to us kids to survive.

Let me back track a little so you have a good understanding of why she eventually fell victim to cancer. In our house the man was king and what he said goes. It didn't matter what the issue was, if he said jump the answer was how high. To give you an example of this I was never baptized because my father told my mother that the boys were his and she could not make the decisions for us. He wanted to groom his sons in the same fashion as him. To be the king and don't take any lip from a woman. It was again another power trip on his part.

"Make them men," he would say.

At any cost we were going to be tough and become the kings of our domain. My father confused discipline with abuse. The more extreme, the more we would become men. He was unable to walk that fine line when it came to punishment. Many times the thought of my father getting angry made me sad because I knew that he was going to take it out on my siblings. Don't forget, when it came to being cruel I was spared whatever twisted game he wanted to play.

No one felt this more than my brother Doug. Doug was twelve, maybe thirteen, and my Father treated him like he was a man in a maximum security prison. It was a daily ritual to see what kind of pain my father could inflict on my brother. Doug had a problem with wetting the bed as many kids do. Thinking about it now, my brother had this problem in response to the way he was being treated. In order to help my brother overcome his problem my father would force him to wear his soiled underwear on his head to humiliate him. Doug was paraded around outside for all to see. My father couldn't leave it in the house. His thinking was that the peer pressure would cause my brother to change his ways. This was the warped thinking that was in my father's head.

It seemed that my father was out to break my brother like a wild stallion and teach him that he will never be the man of the house. I feel there was a lot of fear in my father that Doug would get big enough to fight back, so it was the plan of my father to break him and make him forever submissive to his rule. As an adult I see that his plan worked. I wish Doug had had enough strength to remove himself from the rule of my father.

The abuse did not stop there. My father liked to play mind games while he would punish his children. If you were to get a spanking, that spanking alone would not be enough. He would have my siblings go pick a switch of the tree and bring it back to him. If the switch was not up to his standards he would make them go back and then give you double the lashings. I will never forget seeing the effects those switches would have on bare flesh. Over and over again I would hear the whoosh of the switch followed by a high-pitched smack of the skin. One by one the torn flesh would slowly ooze blood and swell.

My father also had a game he liked to play that was the most damaging in my opinion. My father had a name for it but for some reason I cannot recall what it was. For punishment my siblings would have to stand back from a wall about three feet. They would then have to lean forward and put their hands flat on the wall slightly above their heads. When the command was given everyone would raise up on their tippy-toes and fingertips. There they would stay until he gave the command to stop. This was only a rest.

The command would come again "up", and again they would rise up on their tippy-toes and fingertips. Quickly the tears would come, as this was a very painful torture. Over and over this would happen and over and over the tears would come. Threats of hitting and violence would come if any of them asked to come down before it was time. The pressure it puts on the under-developed joints and muscles is unbearable.

Their arms would begin to shake and tremble out of control. The blood would escape from their fingertips and become numb making it even more painful. This was repeated until their arms were so tired that they collapsed usually slamming into the walls. This was a grueling way to punish children. I can't help but cry as I write this, because I was my father's favorite and I never was subject to this strict torture. I would sit on the couch and watch as this would go on for hours in some cases. I feel as though I owe it to my family to somehow repay the pain I was spared.

I feel selfish to talk about how I was affected by this but it was mental abuse to sit and watch the ones you love being tortured like that. This punishment was also hard on my mother and many times she acted in the defense of her children. When she would come to the defense of her kids she would also feel the wrath of his fists or words. He was a ruler of fear and used it to control and manipulate people to get what he wanted. My father felt no remorse for the way he treated his kids. This is evident by what happened next.

My oldest sister was riding a skateboard one day and fell, breaking her right arm. There was no time to have a broken arm as she was on the schedule to do the dishes that night. My father made her wash the dishes with a broken arm. My sister stood over the pile of dishes with tears streaming down her face doing her best to not show how much pain she was in. there was no way to hide what she was feeling, it was written all over her face. With every movement came a wince and more tears. She was to stand there and finish her dishes without complaining. This task was carried out under the watchful and controlling eye of my father.

This kind of treatment was not uncommon. It was my father's way of making us tough and carrying out his brand of punishment. Getting hurt in our house was just an inconvenience to him and we often paid the price. There was a time when I got a sixteen-penny nail stuck in my foot. It ran the length of my foot from just below my toes to my heel. We were playing tag in the back yard and in true fashion of an early eighties poor kid I was bare footed. I rounded the corner of the house in a dead sprint crossing the back of the house. My best guess is that the nail was laying flat on the ground. Sliding on the dirt to make a hairpin turn the nail was forced the whole length of my foot. The pain was sharp and quick. In a flash I was limping to the house to get help. Having a huge nail in your foot has a way of sending fear through your body in an instant.

I paused at the back door and gathered myself and dried my tears. I knew if I went into that house crying over something stupid I did, it would spark his anger and someone would have to pay. I sat on the back porch and knew what it was I had to do. If I went to my father I knew he would come down on Doug for not watching me. I pulled my foot up and placed it on the other knee in the figure four position. I grabbed the head of the nail with two fingers and my thumb. The pain pierced me deep in my body. The tears began to flow and my breathing got deep. I wanted to yell for Doug to help me but I had to keep it secret so that way no one would be punished for my actions. Three times I tried and three times the pain grew. I had no choice. I had to go in the house and get help.

I limped into the house and made my way to the dusty old chair where my father was sitting. I could tell by the smell and the Coors can on the coffee table that he had been drinking.

"What the?" is all he said.

I could tell by the look on his face that the rage was building.

"Get the damn pliers out of the drawer," he barked.

There was no sympathy or compassion. I could feel the pliers as he clamped them down on the head of the nail. With one long jerk he pulled the nail out and instructed me not to cry. What was a six-year-old boy to do but cry? I felt every inch of that nail as it was pulled from my flesh. There was no tetanus shot or antiseptic to help aide in the healing process. You guessed it, I never cried. At least not in front of him.

Then there was the time my sister and I made a teeter-totter out of a piece of wood and an old Igloo cooler. (We had a lot of homemade recreational toys. We had an old wooden milk crate that was mounted on the garage that served as our basketball hoop and many times had improvised a ball.) We were standing on the teeter-totter going up and down when I decided to see if I could launch her into the air. My sister fell on the ground striking her knee on a rock. This opened up a large cut on the top of her knee that needed to be stitched up. My sister was given several spankings for getting hurt. Much like the nail in my foot she was scared to get help. She knew there was a consequence for doing something stupid. As you can see, my father was not the most caring parent in the world. As you will find out he was an evil husband too.

The Last Morning

The abuse on my mother was the most painful to watch. The sicker she became, the more ramped up the abuse. I don't know what would possess a man to beat on a woman that was dying from cancer but I watched it happen right in front of my face. More than once, us kids were forced to sit outside and watch and listen as he beat on her. It was kind of like watching a horror movie where all you could see were shadows. We could hear the shouting and see the silhouettes in the window. One particular fight still stands out when I think back to those days. Those shadows are still burned into my mind. Not necessarily because of the fight but because of the fact that my mother was in a wheelchair and was too sick to defend herself.

I clearly remember one cold night when I was overcome with hate and wanted to kill my father. I was seven and I had thought out a plan to stab him in the heart when he had passed out drunk. I had a plan and I spent the next few days planning and trying to psych myself up. The thoughts had plagued my mind for some time. I caught myself staring at a large knife as it sat on the counter. It was the graphic vision I had of actually carrying out my plan that shook me back to reality and made me very scared, not only of my father but of my thoughts as well.

I don't even think there had to be a reason for him to beat her. He just had a need to prove his worth, and violence was his only way. Most of the time it was because he was drunk and when he would drink this feeling of power caused rage in him. There didn't have to be a reason for his actions. I know it was how he dealt with his own issues but it caused me to hate him at the time and I wanted him gone. If he made someone feel intimidated he felt like he was the king and that made him feel better about himself. As I have stated before my father was not a big man but very strong. When he was drunk he would exhibit rage and lash out physically.

Once he punched out a security window in the front door that resulted in many stitches. This was a thick window with a wire screen pressed between two panes of glass. Another time he slashed open a waterbed because he wanted to prove a point. My father grabbed a butcher knife from the kitchen and plunged it deep into the bed. I feel he used this as a way to instill fear into all of us. It was almost like he was saying "this could happen to you if you don't fall in line".

As cancer began to ravage and overtake my mother's body, he became irritated and the abuse on my mother increased. It was as if he was doing it to her just to relieve his stress. After treatments when she was weak he would taunt her because she was too weak to defend herself. Once, when she was in a wheelchair, she had to use the restroom and needed assistance. My father got up and acted like he was going to help her.

Sitting on the couch I could see my father walk over to her and take the grips of her wheelchair in his hands and begin to push her to the bathroom. I didn't pay much attention to his actions because I had finally thought he was going to show her the smallest amount of love and concern. Instead he wheeled her to the doorway of the restroom and left her there. Knowing she could not get up and help herself he took a macabre joy in her suffering. If we tried to help, we would get punished.

She sat there and cried for help over and over again. He said, "If she wants to get better she would get up and help herself." This kind of action was torture on us all. The cries of my mother would crush and devastate my heart and I recall the painful lump that would settle in my throat. I wanted so much to help her. I know all of us kids were hurt and crushed at the way our mother was being treated. How could someone be so mean to a woman who is dying of cancer? I began to have more thoughts of killing my father but now my mother was dying and what would happen to us if they both were gone?

There were times that he would wheel her around the house and pop wheelies with her in the wheelchair. This was the action of a sick man. He couldn't care less for life so I know he did not care for my mother. My father never wanted her to get better and did his part in making it very hard on her. This was no more evident than when she started to show improvements.

In fact, the letters she wrote spoke of how much better she was feeling. This news only made my father angrier. I feel that he was ready to move on without her and having her start to make a recovery only fueled his fire and stoked his rage. In the most sinister of intentions he refused her any more treatments. Looking back now, it is clear to me that my father was a cruel and heartless man who was only out for his own gain and happiness. The simple fact is that he wanted her gone and did not care how it happened.

She quickly deteriorated and became very sick. The cancer was eating her body from the inside out. There were times when she was so sick that she could not dress the open sores on her breast. The cancer had eaten through her left breast and required constant attention. She was very weak and required help, of which the responsibility fell on the kids. At this point my father had totally written her off. He refused to help at all and was drinking heavily.

It was up to us four kids to help her out and take care of the family. This responsibility fell squarely on the shoulders of my oldest sister Laurie. She would cook, clean and do dishes all the while taking care of us younger kids. Needless to say her childhood had been stripped away from her and she was thrust into adulthood. Times were hard for all of us. We knew that our mother was going to die and there was nothing we could do about it. We knew that no matter how hard we tried that someday soon she would be gone and even though we had a father we would be left to fend for ourselves.

One Saturday night in March, all seemed to be going as any other night. Dinner was served and cleaned up, we had our baths, and began to go to bed. The hide-a-bed was pulled out for my mother. That is where she slept because she was too disgusting to sleep with my father; at least that was what he said. We all retired to our beds for the night. I am not too sure why but I went to sleep with my mother. I m not sure if I will ever get an answer. As I recall we took turns sleeping with her so we could help if we needed to. However, I remember being wakened in the morning and told to go to a neighbor's house. There was no hiding that something tragic had happened and I could feel a tingle that started at the top of my head and traveled the entire length of my body. Walking across the street I could sense the sorrow pouring off my sisters. My brother was blank with no expression on his face. This was it. I knew what had happened. My mother was gone and now life was going to change for the worse. I was a month away from my seventh birthday the day my mother passed away and left the pain of this world behind.

I have vivid memories of sitting on my sister's lap as we were told our mother was gone. It was hard to understand at first but as time wore on, the permanent nature of the situation started to take hold of me. I wanted my mommy. Why did she leave? I wanted more than ever to feel her pull me close and speak softly to me like she had so many times before. I was too young to grasp what had just happened. I began to revert back to when I was small and all I wanted was to give her a kiss on the cheek and tell her it was going to be ok but she was gone. I still feel the pain and immense sorrow of that day. What was going to happen to us now? The only comfort we had was gone.

The following days seem to be a blur but I do remember meeting my Aunt Judy and Uncle Steve and going to The Star of India. That is an old ship in the San Diego Harbor. I also have memories of the family at a visitation for my mother. Later as an adult I was able to get pictures of that day. The look of horror on the faces is enough to make your stomach turn. My sister Tammy looked so terrified as well as Doug. I would learn why they were so scared later in life. My life was devastated and I knew in my heart that I would now have to totally rely on my brother and sisters if we were to make it in life.

I relived the day my mother died over and over for many years. I would replay the events of that day so I could remember my mother. It took me many years to get to the point where I would not break down and cry uncontrollably. This was the last clear memory of my mother that I had and I was willing to hold on to that day instead of forgetting her. I know this kind of sounds weird but at my age it was all I had. After some time I was able to remember some of the good times with my mother. My mother was overweight and I remember that her hands were pudgy but so soft. Her touch made me feel warm and I truly missed my Mom. It was a traumatic time and I was young with not much help in the grieving process. This caused me to go into a shut down mode. We didn't talk much about it so I attempted to work it out on my own. I was seven years old and not able to grasp the gravity of the whole thing.

I did my best and so did my siblings to deal with the changing world we lived in. This is at the time I could honestly say I had to start to fend for myself. Not with the material things but the intangible things. I could not control my emotions and this equated into anger. Don't get me wrong, I had my brother and sister but we all were in survival mode and doing what we could to make it in life. I was in need of that motherly touch, and no matter how hard people tried it did not suffice.

After a small service my mother was taken to Cottonwood, Arizona to be buried. (I believe her mother and brothers drove her back). There was no big service or a long procession, just family and some friends my mother had made along her journey. I remember the color, powder blue everywhere and I would confirm this later when I received pictures of that day. There is one picture that stands out more than the rest. The four of us are sitting on a couch in the funeral home. I again was being held and comforted by my oldest sister. The look on our faces told the story loud and clear. We had just lost the one thing in our lives that we wanted most. We were left alone to deal with the violent tendencies of my father and his inability to provide for us. At my young age I was keen to the fact that we were destined to a life of hell as long as we were with my father. My siblings had that look on their faces for a completely different reason. I hope someday that those reasons will be shared.

The long Trip

Shortly after the memorial service we were told that we were moving to Ohio. I don't know the time frame but I think it was only a few days or a week. Something very strange happened though. When we left, my oldest sister Laurie did not come. Being a young kid I did not pay much mind to it. I just took my father's answer and left it at that. I knew something was wrong due to the fact that we left so quickly. I don't remembering packing anything of value and we left in a car. No moving van or return trip required. Just grab some of your personal things and go.

We started off on our cross-country trip and I was feeling happy. I think it was because we were leaving the place where so much bad stuff had taken place. I remember it was a long trip. Along the way I fell asleep and got gum stuck in my hair. I also remember White Sands, New Mexico. We also stopped in Missouri to see my Uncle Ronnie. Things were fun and exciting at this point. It was definitely a lot better than Lemon Grove. I wanted to be happy and I began to listen to my father and warm up to him. He talked about the stress he felt and this was the cause of his actions and I believed him. He was clever and he knew no matter what I would always come back to his side.

Once we arrived in Ohio we settled in with my grandmother. She seemed to be pretty nice and made us feel welcome. The town we lived in was a lot nicer than where we had just come from, which is not saying much. My cousin lived two houses down and we made friends real quick. I was now seven and began to feel like things would get "normal". It's funny how things seem to change so quickly in my life. One day, not long after we got there and after a sandlot baseball game, we were all sitting on the front porch of my grandmother's house when two black cars pulled up. It was a warm day but a cool wind blew when these cars rolled to a stop. Please keep in mind that I have been treated differently than my other siblings and I once again think my father is a god. I was never subject to the hell the other kids felt. I was his buddy and he was mine. For this reason the next few events were devastating for me as well. I watched in amazement as the events unfolded in front of me. Just like in a movie, two black, non-descript cars pulled up in front of the house. Four men got out and asked to see my father.

The men were shown in and immediately placed my father in handcuffs and read him his rights. There was not much talking and there was no resisting. My father simply hung his head and walked out of the house. As my father and the men walked by us kids there was not even a goodbye from him. I used to think he was ashamed of his actions but I know now that he was just mad that he got caught. With that, they placed my father in one of the cars and drove away. No goodbye or explanation. I stood there and watched them drive away.

I was confused and scared. Oddly, there were no emotions pouring out of my brother or sister. At the time it never crossed my mind, but looking back I now see why. For the first time in their lives they were free from him and his reign of terror. I would not see my father again for almost three years.

My father was extradited back to California where he was charged and convicted of the sexual molestation of my oldest sister. I was never given an explanation as to why my father was arrested and it would be many years before I would know the truth. As a result of my father's arrest, legal guardianship was given to my grandmother. Reflecting back now as an adult I know this was something she did not want to do.

It was hard on my grandmother to take on three kids. There simply was not enough money, energy, or patience left in her. As a kid it never crossed my mind that things were not a hundred percent at grandma's house. She simply was just not in a position to take on the responsibilities of three kids. I knew she was poor and that was just a way of life.

There is a story I tell my kids when they complain about not having the latest fashions. We had no choice when it came to clothes shopping. This meant that we got to shop at the Family Dollar Store for clothes. One year was really bad. I needed shoes and money was real tight. I went with my grandmother to the store to shop for shoes. Once there I knew I was not going to be happy. There they were; powder blue xj900's with plastic soles. These were the cheapest shoes in the store. They set my grandmother back three dollars. I still have a little resentment over those shoes; they would cause me a lot of teasing and grief.

When I got home I took the worst teasing I have ever experienced in my life. That night we had a street football game and I decided to try out my new shoes. On the very first play of the game I knew that those shoes would not be good. Remember they had plastic soles? The first time I tried to stop I slid all the way to the side of the road. It was like playing on ice. I was the butt of many jokes, but it was a fact of life that I grew to accept.

Being poor was part of my childhood and it was not more evident than at mealtime. We had a schedule of breakfast, lunch and dinner. We had oatmeal for breakfast every day. Ramen noodles for after school snacks and a small rotation of dinners. Wednesday night by far was the worst: liver and onions! Grandma was old school and there was no leaving the table till all your food was gone. We had very creative ways to dispose of unwanted Wednesday night dinner. That was the only night I begged to wear a button up shirt with a chest pocket.

Despite the lack of money and resources my grandma did the best she could do. She called on outside sources to help occupy our time and keep us out of the house. The biggest form of distraction was the local Boys Club. We spent almost every free moment there after school. It was a dime to get in and we could stay till they closed at 9 o'clock. We were able to shoot pool, play foosball, and do arts and crafts. The club was the best thing for us because it supplied us with good wholesome activities that kept us off the streets. In a small town it is easy to get into trouble so I credit the Boys Club with giving the opportunity to stay safe and productive as a kid. I learned many good values at the Boys Club.

If the weather was hot we spent our time at Eastview Pool, the local community pool. We were always in the water if it was summertime. Our day would start out with swimming lessons early in the morning. Later when the pool opened to the public we were back in the water playing with friends and eating junk food from the concession stand. My favorite buy from the concession stand was the Chico Sticks. That crunchy peanut buttery stick was the highlight of many summer days. For three years our life followed this schedule, and I actually had grown comfortable and kind of fond of that lifestyle. By the time I was ten years old I had become a certified lifeguard. Swimming was a way of life that helped to keep me on the straight and narrow.

We were happy kids for the time we were with Grandma. She was fun to be with but had a mean streak a mile wide. This was no more evident than when I was caught stealing a pack of gum from the local corner store. It was called the Five Points store because it was at the intersection where five roads crossed. I was there with my cousin and we were daring each other to steal something. I was the dumb one that decided to stand up and take the challenge.

I slowly walked up to the rack of gum and carefully selected the one I was going to take. I reached out my trembling hand and took possession of that sweet treat. Without missing a beat I put the gum into my pocket. My heart raced, as now I was a criminal and living the dangerous life. We paid for three pieces of penny candy and began to walk out of the store. By now I could feel sweat as it beaded up on my forehead. I was truly scared and just wanted to get out of there.

My cousin walked out first with me hot on his trail. I was so scared I began to shake and my steps became very heavy. This is probably why there was a gap between my cousin and me. No matter, because was out and I began to regain my composure. I did it! I stole some gum. I was about to breathe easy when my cousin turned and shouted, "Did you take it"? That was the downfall of our crime.

I looked over my shoulder to see the clerk had walked behind us to catch a breath of fresh air. He heard everything and knew we had stolen the gum. The clerk was a large man and his hand swallowed my shoulder as he pulled me backwards into the store. Without a second thought my cousin ran from the store leaving me there to take the full brunt of the punishment.

I was taken into a back room of the store where the clerk called the owner and the police. Holy crap! I knew I was going to go to jail and have to go home to my Grandma. I was dead and I knew it. The police showed up and I felt as though I had just swallowed a watermelon. I couldn't breathe and now I was sweating out of control. The police showed up and placed me in handcuffs. It was at this point I was crying like a baby with a messy diaper. The owner of the store showed up and began to talk to the police officer. They were discussing what to do with me. It started out that I was going to juvenile hall and charged with theft. Then the owner took mercy on me and decided to make me clean the parking lot for a week as a way to pay restitution for my actions.

The handcuffs were taken off and I was free to go but the worst of my punishment was yet to come. I had to go home to tell my Grandma. She already knew but I still had to face her. When I got home she was sitting at the dinner table waiting for me to tell her what happened. Before I could start talking she swung and hit me square in the face with her house slipper. She was prepared for me and unleashed a whirlwind of beatings on me. I will never forget how agile that old woman was when she got that angry. I couldn't complain because I deserved it. I cleaned that parking lot for the whole week and hated every minute of it.

Welcome Back

Like many things in my early life, the happy times seem to end abruptly. This is true with the boys club and swimming. Time was served and my father returned home from prison and had his own ideas of what was good for us. He rented a house down the street from my grandmother and we moved in with him. Just like before my father didn't care for anything or anybody. It was all about him and soon he began doing as he pleased and forgot he had kids.

Something very strange happened that I would not make sense of till I was an adult. My sister Tammy did not make the move, so my father, brother, and I lived at the other end of the street from my grandmother. Of course the house was dirty and full of cockroaches. Back to our old life it would seem. There was not an ounce of happiness in that house that I can remember. My father quickly went back to his drinking and barely holding down a job.

We did our best as kids to help out but what we could contribute was minimal.

Once my father worked at a transmission shop and we got paid to cut the weeds down. My brother and I worked all day chopping and hauling away weeds. Two bad things happened from this little work adventure. First, my wages were taken from me so we could buy pizza for dinner and second, my brother was covered from head to toe with poison ivy. His skin was extremely red and swollen. He was miserable and got no sympathy from my father. The only response was a low laugh followed by, "I guess you will never do that again dumb ass".

We began to dwindle and get into trouble after awhile. There was no structure in our house. There were no real rules to speak of. I remember that my brother was smoking marijuana and hitting acid. Once when I was left alone at the house I scoured my brother's room to find the marijuana and get some for my friends and me. Well I found it and took enough for one joint. By the looks of things my brother had quite the little business going. He had his plants growing and had all the necessary tools to harvest, dry, and sell his little crop. Drugs were popular in this small town in the middle eighties.

For fun on two occasions my brother and his friends gave me a hit of acid to watch me trip out while I felt the effects it had on my body. I don't recall what I saw or did but one time the trip was severe and I fell hard several times in the alley. The falls were serious enough that we had to pick rocks out of my knees that had embedded themselves there during the falls. It hurt like hell and for the first time in my life I was really mad at my brother.

This kind of stuff was very commonplace where we lived. At a back to school party my brother was having some guys thought it would be funny to see what I was like drunk. There is no memory of what I drank or how much. I do, however, remember walking up on an old weight bench having wet myself after I passed out. My father was nowhere around to set rules or even protect his kids from things like I described. The night of the party he never came home. I was ten and free to do as I pleased. I had smoked pot and taken acid and I am willing to bet he never found out. He was too busy worrying about how he was going to get his next drink or what woman he could pick up. His kids were always second place. Due to his actions, we kids were put in some pretty bad situations.

This leads me into a story that still to this day makes me sick to my stomach. If my sons were ever put in this position it would set off a fire in me that no one could put out. At the age of ten I was slapped with a restraining order from my best friend and his parents. As fate would have it his name is Bobby too. The story goes like this:

Bobby, my sister and I were in this large park named Crawford Woods. It was where we kids spent a lot of time. We had decided to go to the 'Bowl'. I was basically a large crater in the earth where kids would ride their bikes and hang out.

When we arrived some older kids met us; the neighborhood bullies. We knew who they were and we did not pay much attention to them as our brother was a popular kid and we got a pass all the time because of this little fact. On this day things were different. They did not care who our brother was. A couple of the girls who were much bigger than us all began to pick on my sister Tammy. They wanted her to fight but she did not fight back when they began to push her. I'm not going to lie I was scared to death of what might happen. Without warning the girls threw several quick punches all of them landing on Tammy's face and head. The whole exchange took less than three seconds. When they were done her face was red and swollen. Her nose was bleeding and began to drip onto the front of her shirt.

"Come on Tammy," I yelled to her. "Let's get out of here."

As we turned to leave, the biggest girl grabbed Tammy by the collar of her shirt and yanked her back and pinned her arm behind her almost as if she was a criminal being hauled off to jail.

"This bitch is coming with us," she said. "If you want her back, come and get her at my house you little pussy."

They took Tammy and walked away. I was terrified and began to cry. What was I going to do? If I went home mostly likely Tammy would get a beating, or if my father went to get her he would without a doubt beat her when we got home. I tried to find my brother but he was nowhere to be found. I knew what I had to do. I had to go to the house to get my sister.

Bobby and I mustered up enough courage to walk to the house where my sister was being held captive. Once there, we were motioned to the old run down detached garage that was beside the house. We stepped into the dark building and let our eyes adjust. There, at the other end, was my sister Tammy tied to an old chair. Her nose had stopped bleeding but the evidence of the day's events still stained the front of her shirt. I ran over to release her thinking that it was a game and this would soon be a memory. I was wrong.

"You won't leave here alive you little punk unless you do what we say." By this time my fear was turning into anger.

"Fuck you," I shouted, almost hoping they would jump me so Tammy and Bobby could go free.

I could feel the anger slowly fester up and begin to turn to rage. I did have a temper, and when pushed hard enough I could unleash hell's fury.

"Is that so," one of the boys asked. "Get her," he commanded.

With that, they punched Tammy again and sat her back into the chair. Pointing to Bobby they ordered me to beat him up.

"No," I shouted, and began to move towards Tammy.

I knew then it was no joke and I needed to do something. I wanted my sister to be safe but I could not fight my friend. I think Bobby knew this too, so without warning he took a swing at me just glancing my shoulder. Almost as though someone reached inside and turned on a switch, I snapped. I began to see red and my pulse was about to redline. I swung back as hard as I could, landing my punch on his left temple. I think this dazed him a little because he never threw another punch. One after another I let my fist fly. I could feel the bone structure of his face every time I hit him. My only thought was about Tammy and keeping her safe. The blood began to cover his face and my fist. This seemed to only fuel the fire that was inside me.

By this time his body had collapsed and I was swinging at everything. There was no stopping me. I could hear Tammy yelling and I began to panic. I swung harder trying to please the crowd so I could leave and go home.

With a deep thud followed by a high-pitched ringing I stopped the flurry of fists. The biggest boy in the group got scared and tried to pull me off. When this did not work he drew back and punched me in the right side of my head. It felt like a bomb went off in my head. When the smoke cleared, Bobby lay in the middle of the floor bloody and crying. The crowd ran off and I was left there with my beaten up sister and my best friend that I just pounded. Through my tears I saw a figure standing in the doorway of the garage. It was Chris. Chris was Bobby's older brother. Someone from the crowd got scared and ran to get Chris to come help.

I began to cry even harder. I was scared and ashamed of what I had just done. How can you explain what happened? Chris quickly scooped up Bobby and took him home. Tammy and I went home and cleaned up. We told my Grandma that Tammy had fallen and all was well. We lied. It was all messed up. Later that night a police officer came to the door and handed my father a piece of paper. It was a restraining order. I had sent Bobby to the hospital to get stitches and to repair his broken nose. I am not sure all that happened with Bobby but I should have gone to jail or something. We never talked about it again and the order was lifted. I never said I was sorry, and it was as though he forgave me and understood what had happened. Bobby and I were always tight and we stuck together till the day I moved away.

Living with my father was an adventure every day. With not much supervision and a father who was absent most of the time, it was easy to make poor decisions. Many times we needed a parent to make a decision or lay down a law. It just was not there. We were living our own wild west. I think he wanted friends and not kids.

My father had a warped sense of what children our age should be doing to occupy our time. I can remember a ritual my father started every Friday. That was to go to the drive thru liquor store buy himself some beer and his kids some wine coolers. We would then drink our beverages while we went on long drives in the countryside. It was common for my sister and me to drink our six packs of wine coolers while we went on our trip. To make things even more twisted my father would let me sit on his lap and control the car while he would see how fast he could get the car to go. I remember how proud he was the day we hit one hundred miles per hour together. I had just turned eleven and he thought this was the greatest thing ever. Looking back now as a father it makes me sick to know he was so careless and had no regard for his kids' safety.

We had other rituals, like going to the bar and he would leave me with a fist full of quarters to play pinball while he got drunk. This type of behavior went on for about the next year. There were many times when I was left to be the adult. Alcohol had totally taken over my father and he was burning bridges left and right. His behavior was causing him to lose many friends and he was becoming quite the village idiot.

Doing what he pleased and not thinking about others was a way of life for my Father. I was nine and we were riding down the street in Reading, Ohio just outside Cincinnati. It was just an average day with no real reason to be angry. The sun was shining and the birds were singing. By all accounts it was a great day. We had just pulled up to a red light and got into the left hand turn lane. We were behind a car waiting for the light to change to green. The radio was on and we were listening to country music. Again, there was nothing to be upset about. The light turned green and nothing happened. The car in front of us did not move. Instantly my father's rage exposed it's self. The horn on the car did not work, so my father just pulled around the right side of the car to go around. As we crept alongside the car my father yelled out, "Move, you fucking nigger."

With that, he completed the left turn and proceeded down the street. About a mile down the road we were stopped at another light. I was sitting there, not paying much attention to anything when a mind-shaking explosion went off on my left side. The flash was blinding and I could feel the heat as it warmed my face. In a split second my world went silent and blood splattered on my shoes and lower left side. As quickly as it went silent, all hell broke loose.

"Fuck you cracker," was all I heard as I was thrown back in my seat from the rapid acceleration of the car. Reality began to set in and I started to figure out what happened. At the red light, the man that my father yelled at had followed us, and once we stopped he exited his car. He walked up to the driver's side of our car and fired one shot into the car striking my Father in the left leg just above the knee. The bullet passed completely through his leg and embedded in the floorboard of the car. I could not hide the terror I felt. I told my Father to pull over so I could pee behind a dumpster. I wanted to play the tough guy role but he knew what I needed to do. Once behind the dumpster I puked like I had never before my life. I was scared to death. I had just witnessed my Father getting shot and I was right there less than two feet away.

I jumped back into the car and it was obvious that he was in a lot of pain and needed help. I began to cry and pleaded with him to go to the hospital before he got worse. My father looked at me and told me to be strong, that I needed to make sure I got him to his girlfriend's house.

"Go to the hospital please," I again begged.

"I can't!" he said. "I have a warrant out for my arrest and if I go to the hospital they will call the police and I am on parole."

I was crushed. I was young and knew my Father was going to die. Blood had covered the driver's side of the car and his girlfriend was over thirty minutes away. I made a decision that no matter what I was going to get him help. When we started or trip home he seemed fine. As time progressed I had to help him steer the car. All those times he took us out to drive with him actually was paying off this time. By the time we reached his girlfriend's house he was ready to pass out. I ran upstairs to get her to help, as he could not walk by himself at this point. We got him upstairs and took him to the bathroom to dress his wounds. We laid him in the bathtub and pulled his pants off. Just above his knee were two holes one slightly bigger than the other. We both pressed on a hole with a towel for a few minutes to stop or slow the bleeding.

Once the bleeding had slowed his girlfriend poured alcohol or peroxide on the wounds to clean them. The yelling was too much and I again began to feel sick and needed to leave the room. I ran outside to the backyard and fell to my knees clutching my stomach from the pain I felt. I stayed outside till his girlfriend came down to check on me. She knelt down beside me and told me he was in bed sleeping and he should be ok. I felt her hand touch the back of my head and gave me a gentle tug. I collapsed into her and broke down crying as she held me tight. I could only think about my mother and how I wanted it to be her holding me in that backyard. Then my thought turned to my father and how I wanted him to take me far away from this place so we could be happy.

Here We Go Again

One day a funny thing happened. My father came home and it was obvious that he had been drinking due to the slurred speech and angry tone in which he spoke. He had a plastic bag in his hand that was full of spray paint cans. Those cans of spray paint were cans of primer to paint our car. This was his attempt to hide his car.

To this day I am still not sure why he needed to hide but we all pitched in to help primer the car. There was certain haste in the way he wanted this done. We soon found out why. He told us to pack up our clothes and some of our belongings and get ready to move to Florida. To any young kid moving to Florida was the greatest thing in the world and I was no different. Yes it was odd that we were leaving in such a haste, but what did I care, it was Florida.

Soon after we were on our way to Florida in a primer black 1979 Ford Grand Torino. It was my sister Tammy and I along with my father driving south to the land of sun and beaches. My brother decided to stay back and not make the trip. He was getting older and I think he was afraid to go to Florida with my father. He had settled into life in Ohio and I don't think he could handle being uprooted again.

We had some trouble on the way down that prolonged our arrival a little, but for the most part it was fun trip. We got to see places we had never seen before like Tennessee and Georgia. It was in Atlanta, Georgia that we encountered some trouble. While on the freeway we blew out a tire and it was getting late. After a few hours and a little begging and pleading we were back on the road. We stopped for the night close to the state line and slept in the car at a rest stop. We were up early the next day and soon we reached the Florida state line and there were smiles all around. You could feel the excitement in the air. The land looked so green and the wildlife was abundant. I couldn't wait to see the beach and swim in the ocean.

Before we could settle down and calm ourselves we were in a Holiday Inn in Orlando. It was a really nice place for a kid from Ohio. The weather was warm and the trees were awesome. We would swim in the big pool and tan in the sun. Finally my life was making a turn to the good side. For the first time in my life I was feeling happy and like a kid should feel. Things got better because my brother was on his way down to be with us and help out my father to get us all set up. Once my brother got to Orlando I truly felt safe, so it was devastating when he left one week later.

As it turns out he was there to try to take us back to Ohio but my father would have none of it. My brother left after a fight with my father and I would not see him for a couple of years. Once my brother left, the happiness and fun left our little family.

We moved out the Holiday Inn and moved into an old dirty run down motel. My father was not working and things were getting tight financially. The motel was cheap but we got what we paid for. There were stains on the wall and oddly enough there was a faint sour odor that reminded me of San Diego. We were not eating well and it seemed that we had returned back to the old ways of life.

I would soon suffer another loss that would change my life. By now I was used to things changing and for the most part change was never good.

My sister got on a bus and headed to North Carolina to live with my oldest sister and her family. This was the first time I truly felt alone in life. I was scared and not sure what the future held for me. I did my best to be strong and act like it was going to be ok but I knew I was in for some long, hard years. Now without my brother or sister I was really left to take care of myself. I had no help so I decided that I would have to do it alone.

While living in the motel we met a family that was living there as well. It was a couple and their two girls. They lived two doors down from us and they became our friends and taught us the way of the streets. They were a watered down version of gypsies. He traveled to places like Mardi Gras to find work for a few days. They introduced us to the Coffee House. This was a soup kitchen where we could eat for free every night. It was real hard to adjust to this kind of life. I have always been poor, but let's face it these people were homeless. Even though life had been hard and we made sacrifices, we never had to go without or have to stand in line to get free food. We were at that point. If you were to take away the dirty motel, we would, for all intents and purposes, be homeless. We had nothing and there were no plans to change that.

This became an everyday thing and I think it made it easy for my father to not go get a job. He would fill his days with sitting around and talking about how great he was to the family we befriended. If we needed money he would leave me with the family and go work as a day laborer where he would get paid the same day. This was his temporary way of fixing things. It became clear to me at the age of eleven that I was not going to have a good childhood. It was this time I knew my childhood was gone and I knew I would not have a common life.

My eyes were opened wide the day that my father came home and told me that we were going to move out of the motel and live in the car. At first I thought he was joking but we soon started to pack what little belongings we had in the trunk of the old primer black car. At this point in my life I couldn't help but feel we were totally lost and felt like we were in a spot that could not be fixed.

The first night we slept in the car was the worst by far. We drove out of the city limits and pulled into a rest stop on the side of the highway. We found a spot that we thought we would be left alone and settled in for the night. We found out real quick what a challenge sleeping in the car was going to be. A few hours after we fell asleep there was a knock on the window. Flashlights filled the car and commands to "wake it up" came from outside the car. It was the police and they wanted us to move on because this particular rest stop was a favorite spot of the homosexual culture. This was also the same time a serial killer was stalking the state rest stops.

We drove back into the city looking for a spot to sleep. We found a dead end alley by the old motel where earlier that day we lived in. We again lay down to sleep and again we were woken up by the police and made to move. This is how every night was for us and it made it hard for us to get a good night sleep.

When the morning would come we would find a place to eat a little. Usually it was a shared meal at McDonalds or a small box of cereal from a hotel vending machine. Then my father would go to his day labor job and leave me to roam the streets all day alone. I was eleven and left to fend for myself on the streets of Orlando. I would keep myself busy by playing at the park or I would visit the family that we had met at the hotel.

I got to know a lot of people who were also on the streets and that would help pass the time. This was my routine for quite some time. I had become skilled at street life. I had to be because it is easy to be taken advantage of if I let my guard down. I was learning how to take care of myself and live the ways of the world. In short I was becoming a hard little kid.

Nothing or no one scared me. I hung around a lot of homeless people who befriended me and taught me many valuable things. Living on the streets came easy for me. I guess it's because as kids we got use to taking care of ourselves and we knew how to survive.

I developed many skills on the streets and I used them to my advantage. I learned to steal from the store and not get caught. I was able to get things that my father could not or would not get me. I also developed a way with my words. I would lay a hard luck story down on some of the street people I became friends with and they would give me a dime or quarter. I found out if I was to do this several times a day and save my money for a few days I could treat myself to an ice cream or a real meal. Of course I did not tell my father because I was afraid that he would take it for himself or make me give it back. I developed a scam that pulled money out of the hands of the people that begged to get it in the first place. I never came to a conclusion as to how I felt about that. I do feel bad that I was getting it from people in my own situation but to tell the truth they should have had their guard up better.

I was beginning to generate a lot of money and what I mean by a lot was about three to four dollars every other day. Every third or so while my father was at work I would take my earnings to this mom and pop restaurant that only served all you can eat shrimp. I can still see the pile of fried shrimp as it sits in front of me. This was the only time I felt some sort of normal. I was proud that I was able to provide for myself, and to eat food that had flavor seemed to restore some faith that things might turn out ok.

The times when I was not treating myself or stealing I was at the park. This particular park was my favorite because it had a beautiful lake in the middle of it and big trees around the edge. I would spend most of my time here while I waited for my father to get off of work. If I was lucky enough there would be this old man there that I had become friends with. He would bring an extra fishing pole and let me sit and fish with him. He was a New Yorker that had moved down after he retired and wanted to fish. As it turns out that he was not set up for retirement and lived in a pretty poor part of town. This is why this lake was his fishing spot. Never once did I not enjoy my time fishing with the old man. That is all I ever knew him as was the 'old man'. He was aware of what my situation was and he kept an extra eye on me. When it was time for me to meet my father he would grab the pole out of my hands and tell me to run along. Every time as I would turn to leave he would mumble, "now I can get some goddamn peace." He was my friend and he thought I was in a bad spot and wanted to make it a little better. One day I searched the park and the lake but there was no sign of the old man. Several days passed and still no old man. I wrote it off as just another here today gone tomorrow thing that happens in my life.

When my father finished work I would meet him at the old motel and we would head off to the Coffee House for dinner. After dinner we would go buy some beer and just hang out in the parking lot of the motel till it was time to find a spot to sleep. Night after night and day after day this was the routine. After some time we became known to the police and they were putting pressure on my father to get me off the streets.

We were directed to a homeless shelter where we could get food and a place to sleep. Like most things in my life, this too became something of a hassle. We had to be checked in by 6:00pm and checked out by 5:00am. This was hard because there was limited room and my father did not get off till 5 pm or later and by the time we got to the shelter the chances of us getting in were slim.

If there was a line we would most likely miss the cut off and a lot of the times we did miss out. Once inside the shelter we were able to eat and take a shower. The shower was a bit troubling for me and made me very uncomfortable. There was no privacy and we took showers ten at a time. As a young kid I was very uneasy taking showers with nine other men. Not to mention we were not living with the most clean and sanitary people. Sometimes the water would run brown on the floor if there was a person that had been out for a few weeks and this was he was his first shower.

The building itself was old and run down. There were water stains running down the walls and there was a smell that is real hard to describe. The best way to give a visual would be to describe it as a spoiled sour fish smell. The bunks we slept on consisted of plastic mattresses covered by a sheet that did nothing to protect us from the cold of the mattress. Pillows were small and often carried the smell of the previous user. By far the worst thing I had to endure was the long nights of noises that came from the surrounding bunks. Like it was clockwork there would be the guy who sounded as if he was dying from pneumonia and coughed all night. A few bunks over was the guy who felt the need to fart every few seconds. The tossing and turning would become too much to bear. Once, in the bunk next to me there was a Vietnam Vet who had flash backs and dreams all night. His yelling was keeping everyone up and that just led to others adding to the noise. No matter how bad it got I was still glad to be off the street and some place where the police would leave us alone. I knew if we were in the shelter I would stay with my father.

Most of the time I was the only kid in the shelter so I was forced to act like a grown man. If my father was not around I was vulnerable, and one time I was assaulted physically and got roughed up pretty bad. There were two men and they wanted a ring I had found in the park. I was grabbed around the neck and pushed up against the wall. One of the men held a knife up to my face and asked where the ring was. I told him I gave it to a friend in the park. I felt a crushing pain in my side that would have sent me to my knees had I not been pinned to the wall. I had been punched in my left side. I felt the air escape from my side and I began to cry. I was scared and began to panic. The man that punched me told me I was "Gonna die" if I did not give up the ring. I know the ring had no value but I had nothing and that was something I had found and treasured. I gave up the ring and they left me there to cry and shake from my fear. I never told my father because I was embarrassed and I know I would have gotten in trouble for giving up the ring.

We continued to stay at the shelter for some time while my father worked as a day laborer. I would continue to roam the streets and occupy my time. The days are very long when you have no plan and you are just killing time. It was fall and the nights were very cold so when we missed the cut off for the shelter it was a long, cold night too. We had many of these nights due to the fact that my father wanted to drink beer and visit the people from the motel. Sleeping in the car when it was cold was not the easiest thing to do. Most of the time it was so cold that I would just lie there and shiver the night away. I would watch the windows as they began to fog up and distort the lights as they shined through. I pretended that they were Christmas lights and that gave me some comfort. Many nights came and went where we slept in that car. Each time we did, the anger and disdain grew larger. I didn't mind that we were homeless, I guess I just wished I could have been home in Ohio where I was comfortable and had friends.

I began to feel an over powering feeling of loneliness. My family was gone and I really had no friends. Those that I considered my friends were grown men who lived in the shelter or on the street. Those are not the best people to call friends when you are a kid. Why could I not have a normal life? How did it get so messed up? This is what started to consume me. I needed answers. Believe it or not, when I asked my father he told me I needed a little fun to take my mind off such complex things. He must be kidding! Was he really going to let me ride go-carts or go to the batting cages or even play video games? The answer is no! His Idea of fun for we was to go to the bar with him and some of his friends. I was so mad and wanted to just start running and not look back. When we got to the bar I was given a fist full of quarters like I had been given so many times before and told to play the pinball machine. Not even halfway through the quarters my game was interrupted by my father yelling.

Not again, not now. He was fighting again. I don't remember what was said or what happened to set him off but the tone in his voice told me that he was looking for justification and no one was leaving till he got it. I began to walk to my father because of prior experience. I knew to stay close to him or I could get lost in the shuffle when the fight started. As I got about half way a lady that I had seen with my Father grabbed me and we headed for the door. I remember one sentence from that fight. Before the lady and I left the bar my father said, "Hang tight bud. I will be out in a minute." I hated my situation and the life my father led me into, but at that moment I saw him as a John Wayne figure. For that moment I was not scared. I felt as though he was ten feet tall and bullet proof. I left that bar and sat in the parking lot waiting for John Wayne. A few minutes later I heard the high squeal of the police cars as they raced down Church Street towards the bar. At almost the same time my father came bursting out the door full speed to the car.

Without being prompted I followed suit and dove into the backseat of the car. The car laid down some rubber as I flew against the side of the car from the hard left turn. I could see the faint flash of the lights on the roof of the car as we sped off. Sitting in the backseat, I wanted to jump up and make sure my father was all right but I knew that when he was in the heat of the battle that he was better left alone. I could see in the rearview mirror that he was getting a black eye and there was a small amount of blood trickling from nose. I sat back in my seat and thought about when he was shot a few years earlier and how glad I was to not relive that event in my life again. We spent the next few days keeping a low profile and we stayed out of the city. We had become know to the local beat cops and we knew it was best to let this die down. This was not all a bad thing for us. I still looked at my father as my hero and this gave me some time with just him to visit and regain some of the time I had felt I lost by moving to Florida. I was losing my father and it hurt. I know it might be hard to understand, but he was my father and I was his son. Every time things got real bad he knew exactly what to say to bring me back to the fold.

Thanksgiving came, and there we were sitting in the shelter getting ready to have Thanksgiving dinner. I remember watching people walking by on their way to watch a college football game at the stadium where the Citrus Bowl was played. I don't remember if it was the bowl game or not but I sat there wanting to be them so bad. The smiles on their faces and the way they walked without a care in the world made me so jealous. I couldn't help but ask the same question I had been asking all along. Why not me? At that moment I was filled with rage but not because I was not going to the game. I was mad at myself for always complaining that things were too hard and what about me. I sort of began to hate myself at that moment. I wasn't thinking right and I began to take the blame for the things that were happening to us.

I ate turkey, green beans, stuffing, and baked beans. This was the best meal I had eaten in a long time and it seemed to lift the spirits of my father and those around us. As I sat there I began to smile. What was I thinking? I guess that is when I decided that I would never put my kids through this kind of thing. I wasn't smiling because I was happy; I was smiling because it was all I could do to keep from blowing up and causing a scene. I wanted nothing more than to close my eyes and be gone from this place.

We stayed in that shelter for a few more months to get us through the holidays. I was in the middle of an internal battle to do what was right and not let my true feelings show. I was in a place in life I had never been and I had enough. Christmas for me that year was a pack of markers and a stack of napkins. My father gave them to me like I was supposed to be the happiest kid on earth and got angry with me when I did not praise him for it. I sat there in the booth at the Coffee House staring at my present and on the inside I was crushed. We were alone and this was the first time I was without my family for Christmas. My sister Tammy was gone and so was my brother. I could feel the tears well up in my eyes as I sat there trying to hide the way I felt. "Thanks," was all I could get to come out of my mouth. I never opened the markers to use them. I simply gave them to the little girl we knew from the motel. My gesture was confused for an act of kindness but it was out of disgust that I gave the markers away. I hated Christmas that year and I was beginning to hate my father again.

Leading the Prey to the Wolves

The day came when my father told me he had rented a house and we would be moving out of the city. I was excited because living on the street was hard and I needed to get in a home and go to school. I was closing in on almost a year without school. I did go to a school in Orlando but it was for a very short time. I needed to get back to a normal lifestyle and this house was my ticket. We moved to the house but that was it. There wasn't any electricity or running water. There was no furniture or TV. No comforts to speak of. We had to run an extension cord from the neighbor so we could have power for the refrigerator. We would eat bologna for every meal. The bad thing about it was that there was no mayo or mustard or cheese. It was two slices of bread and one slice of bologna. We ate this for weeks on end.

While living at this house there were some changes that would alter my life. It seems that the family from the old motel had split up and the woman whose name is Tammy came to live with us. She brought her two daughters Tiffany and Ginny to live with us. I had no problem with the girls but I did not like Tammy. When she showed up my father kind of forgot that he had a son. I was now left to fend for myself again and somehow I was expected to take care of these girls too. I was used to taking care of myself, but now I had become a father to two girls. I would be left alone with the girls while my father and Tammy would disappear for a day or two.

There was to be trouble that followed with Tammy. One night, the word came down that Tammy's ex-husband was bringing some of his boys down to kill my father. It was told to us that they were going to come and do a drive by or something stupid like that. That whole night the girls and I were huddled in the back of the house waiting for them to show up. Just like many years before lying on the floor in Lemon Grove, we waited. They never showed up but the attempt on my father's life would come later.

We soon moved out of that house and moved back to Orlando. We moved into a tri-plex and I fooled myself into thinking that now was the time that things would get right in my life. Well once again I was wrong! The trouble only got worse.

We were poor, of course, and no adult in the house had a full time job to speak of. I began to steal things and my father would sell them on the street. I would mostly steal bikes. Those seem to be the easiest to resell. I would steal them and then bring them home. From there they were stripped down, parts mixed up and then repainted. This was not all I would steal. I would be sent into grocery stores to steal things for dinner. I guess they thought that they would never suspect a kid of stealing steaks. Stealing became easy and almost fun till one night I did something that caused me to rethink what I was doing. In the apartment next to ours lived a girl that I liked and spent many days with. I knew her apartment as well as mine. One night when there was a bunch of my father's friends over they decided that I should help them break in my friend's apartment because I knew it so well. They were out of town and that would make it so easy. I was afraid to stand up to my father and his friends in fear that they might hurt me. I agreed to help them and we were on our way. Standing on the porch staring at the door I had the thought to just run away. I would tell my father I was scared and they would rob the apartment anyway. This way I could get out of it and not have to rob my friend.

They kicked the door in and we were in the apartment in a flash. I had no time to execute my plan. This pissed me off because I knew how to get into the house by unlocking a certain window. We were only in the apartment for a few minutes because we did not have to search for anything. I knew where everything in the house was. We cleaned out that apartment and sold everything we stole. I felt sick for a week knowing that I had just done this and I knew how they would feel when they came home.

When they returned home they were devastated. We had taken all they owned and sold it like it didn't matter. I wanted so bad to tell but I knew if I did I would be harmed. I was told that I would be opened up if I told what we did. These were street people and I took it serious when they put the threat out there. With all the things I have ever done this is the one thing I wish I could get forgiveness for. They had befriended me when I had none and I led a band of goons into their house and stole their precious things with no regard for their feelings. I know I was a kid and my father should have been the one to get me out of that situation, but let's face it, I was more mature and equipped to handle life than he was.

Before I knew it I was taking care of the two girls and not going to school. I had not been in school for over a year at this point and I had filled the father role for these two girls. I was cooking and cleaning and trying to keep up the chores so my father would be pleased when he decided to come home. It was my job to change diapers and bathe the girls. If they fell down I was the one giving them comfort and dressing their wounds. When my father was not home I would make sure all was good at home while Tammy sat around and complained about everything. Tammy was a large woman and not much for doing much at all. She never worked and never contributed to the household duties and chores. Our days were filled with a lot of TV watching and utter nothingness. Then the day came when she decided to prey on an eleven-year-old boy.

We were sitting watching TV one day when Tammy began to rub her nipples over her sundress. She went out of her way to make sure that I could see her. She lay down on the floor and continued to play with her breast. She told me to come lay by her, and I refused at first. She told me if I didn't she would tell my father that I tried to touch her and have sex with her. I was afraid that if she did tell my father that he would beat me or do something worse. I complied with the command and lay on the floor next to her. She then took my hand and slid it up her dress and placed it on her breast. She asked if I liked what I felt.

I knew what was going on was wrong but I also knew that I could not stop it either. The girls were asleep in the other room and this made Tammy feel comfortable because she decided to pull her dress up and expose herself to me. As she lay on the floor she began to masturbate a little and tease me that I have never touched a real woman before. I said nothing because I was a little afraid and a little confused as to what was happening. Then she picked up a glass of Kool Aid and poured some on her breast and told me to suck it off. I again refused and this made her mad. She again threatened to tell my father if I did not perform this act. I complied with her demand and she took great pleasure in what was going on. It almost seemed like a game to her and it only fueled her persistence when I refused. At this point it is safe to say that her actions could be considered child molestation.

This episode progressed to the point where she forced me to engage in oral sex and intercourse. She took the approach that it would make me a man and my father would be proud of me but when she was finished she told me if my father found out she would blame me and my father would kill me for messing with his woman. As a kid I was terrified and now I have given all control to Tammy. After the first incident she was real comfortable doing what she wanted to. Whenever she wanted to abuse me she knew she could get away with it and knew I would say nothing.

Tammy, being a heavy set woman, came up with this story that she wanted to lose weight and she wanted to do something about it. Knowing that my father would not walk with her, she would ask me to walk with her to lose weight. I knew what was going to happen if I walked with her. When I would refuse she would tell my father to make me go with her so she did not have to go alone. My father would threaten to whoop my ass if I did not go. Not knowing what was about to happen, he would force me to go.

Once on the walk she would find places to hide and perform sexual acts on me or I would have to perform sex acts on her. One particular night she wanted to have intercourse and I refused. This made her very angry and she left me standing on the side of the road while she began to walk back to the house to tell my father, or so I thought. After a minute or so the fear won out and I chased after her to stop her. Once I caught her she told me I had to make it up to her. I said that was fine and that I would do whatever as long as she kept it a secret. She took me to a Porta-Potty on a construction site and made me perform oral sex on her till she felt I had paid her back. I remember lying in bed that night and tears rolled out of my eyes for hours. No sounds or movements, just tears. I was almost twelve and I wanted to die and leave this world. How could someone just ruin a child like this and not have any remorse about it.

The abuse continued for a couple of years. When I was taken from my father and Tammy, she would call and talk about it as though there was nothing wrong with it. To this day I get sick to my stomach when I remember what she did to me.

Spinning Out Of Control

The second and most real attempt on my father's life came on a night as we drove the streets of Orlando. I don't remember why or where we were driving but there were two men in the car with us. I am not sure who the third man in the car was but the man next to me was one of the guys I broke into the apartment with a few months earlier. I believe his name was Larry.

I was sitting in the back seat behind my father who was driving. Larry sat next to me in the back and the third man in the front passenger seat. Larry was a friend of both Tammy and her ex-husband. As I would soon find out he was better friends with her ex-husband. I will never know how my father found out about the plan to kill him but he knew.

At a red light my father made a quick movement and pulled a machete from under the seat. He spun around in his seat and thrust it toward Larry who was less than a foot away from me. The blade slightly cut his shoulder as he flinched from the surprise of my Fathers actions. I could see the intensity in my Fathers eyes as he held the blade tight.

"Don't move or I will cut your fucking head off," was the command.

I was in complete shock, not knowing what was going on and scared that my father was going to kill this guy, or even worse get killed himself. Larry slowly raised his hands and I could tell he was frightened, knowing that he had just made a huge mistake.

"Where is the gun," were the next words spoken.

Larry responded, "under my leg."

My father instructed Larry that today was his lucky day and that because he had his son with him my father was not going to kill him. My father instructed Larry that he was going to get out of the car and start walking. My father told him that if he saw him and I was not with him that he would kill him without question. Larry slowly and carefully eased out of the back seat where it was confirmed he was not lying.

There on the seat of the car lay a black pistol loaded and ready to go. The plan was to wait till the time seemed right and Larry would shoot my father in the back of the head at point blank range. Somehow my father found out and made his preparations for his defense. In the coming days, the realization of the whole thing hit me. What if this plan had been carried out? What if I was part of the plan? This was the second time I had been in the car with my father when an attempt on his life was in play. I could feel myself becoming jaded to life and I seemed numb to all the bad things that happened in my life. I was learning to not feel.

I am not sure if my father would have killed Larry that night and I am glad I didn't find out. I do know that it has always been rumored that my father had killed a man before and from the look he had in his eyes that night I am willing to bet the rumors are true. I do know that if my father had not received word of what was about to happen, he and I possibly would not be alive today.

Life was getting to be too much for me. I was young and I was experiencing things that a kid at my age should never see or do. I had begun to feel guilty about the things that I had done and seen. I was not having a traditional childhood and it was starting to tear me down. I just wanted to go to school and play baseball like the other kids. Why was my life so different and why could I not change it? These were the thoughts that plagued my mind and caused me to become more and more angry with my father and myself. I wanted so bad to just be 'normal' but it was not to be. Things continued down the same path and soon I gave in to the realization that this is what my life was going to be and I could not change it.

Our money situation still had not improved and we needed to get money. The things we did were just stupid. One night I walked outside to get some fresh air because I felt sick. At the other end of the property I saw Tammy giving oral sex to a man that had been introduced to me as a friend earlier in the night. I watched as she finished up and was paid for her services. The next day she took us kids to eat at a restaurant and she was so proud that she worked and was able to feed us. I got in trouble because I would not eat because I knew how she got the money. I was disgusted at what I had witnessed and that was all I could see when I looked at the food on the table. Of course I was a little ungrateful bastard but I just couldn't bring myself to accept what had happened.

We were in need of a lot of money fast so my father had a plan to get it. He and a friend had planted many marijuana plants on some property his friend had. It was time to harvest and all hands had to be on deck. This meant me too. We drove out to pick the marijuana and bring it back to the house. The plan was to dry it out, package it, and sell it. It took most of a day for four of us to harvest it all. When we were done we had four duffel bags jammed full of marijuana. I am not sure how much we had but it is safe to say each bag weighed twenty pounds. As we were heading back into town the wheel bearings went out on that old Grand Torino. We were stranded! My father determined that we should take the bags and walk. It had begun to rain and he thought someone would see a child in the rain walking and stop to pick us up. He was right. The very first car that drove by stopped to pick us up.

This was actually a bad thing because it was a sheriff deputy that stopped. I don't know if my father was dumb or didn't care, but he walked right up and talked to the deputy. Without missing a beat the deputy opened the trunk of his car and we filled it with our bags. We then piled into the car and were driven into town. On the trip into town my heart was racing uncontrollably and I felt sick n the pit of my stomach. What was wrong with this guy? I know he could smell it. We all could. For whatever reason he did not say a word and he almost took us all the way home.

We dried it out and began to sell it. Slowly the amount of stock began to grow, so we piled it up in the hall closet and began to make some real money. I was awestruck at how easy it was to make money selling marijuana. I had just turned twelve and I was selling drugs on the street. Not too long after we picked and dried the marijuana all hell broke loose.

This was the late 80's and you could still rent VCR's from the video store. We would rent them under fake names and sell them to pawn shops. Well, the police had caught on and came to bust Tammy for selling stolen property. When the police came to arrest her, we had all that marijuana in the closet and I was terrified they would find it. The police showed themselves in and began to snoop around the house. As one of them walked down the hall towards that closet my heart was about to pound out of my chest. The sweat began to bead up on my forehead. I wanted to explode when he brushed up against the door of the closet. I bit my lip and squinted my eyes as though I was in pain. A cramp had formed in my stomach and I could feel my lunch working its way up.

"Where is your father?" he asked.

I made up some lie about how my father would be home soon and I would take care of the girls till he got home. I just wanted them to leave and they did. With Tammy arrested and the story spreading, my father could not sell any more marijuana.

Shortly after the arrest we got evicted from the apartment and had nowhere to go. Tammy made arrangements to have us move out in the country with an aunt and uncle. This seemed fun at first, but this too would change for the worse. It was a small house set on a natural canal that connected two lakes. There was an abundant supply of wildlife that made it exciting. I love to fish and this made it possible to do so whenever I wanted. We could also hunt whenever. Life was starting to level out and I began to settle into this life style like so many times before. I still did not go to school and I still took care of the girls while my father would disappear for a day or sometimes two. I never understood the reason why but this behavior of leaving and coming back days later was very common with him.

Eventually Tammy was released from the county jail from the VCR incident and returned to live with us. The day she got back it was the same sexual game as when she had left. I would have to go on a walk with her so she could get her desired sexual fix. Everyday like clockwork this event took place. By this time it had become a daily part of my life and I submitted to it. I had turned into her personal sex slave and I was terrified to say anything about it. Now that we were out of the city and a little secluded it seemed to get more frequent and bolder. The acts of sexual abuse took place wherever Tammy felt the need. I was becoming numb to the whole idea that things in my life were going to change. After awhile I gave up trying to resist her requests. Time and time again I would stare off into space trying to find that happy place that I could escape to. I guess I just felt helpless and allowed it to happen. I was beginning to hate everything. The things that brought me joy now seemed to frustrate me. I didn't want to do anything but sit and watch TV. I felt broken and it was because my innocence was taken and I knew that I had become a statistic.

We then moved to Tampa to live with some other family members of Tammy. I am not sure how they were related but we moved there and the responsibility of taking care of the girls was taken from me for a short time. I was happy because we lived in a house and ate three meals a day. We would not stay long because of the actions of one of the family members. Again I am not sure how he was related. I think he was Tammy's cousin or something. He wanted to take me out for a night fishing trip and I was excited. The night was perfect for a fishing trip. It was not too cold and the sky was clear. We made our preparations and left the house. The boat was loaded and we had enough food for a small feast. We were on our way and nothing could dampen my excitement. Freedom and fun were two things I did not see much of so when I got this chance I took no time accepting the offer.

Quickly I became confused because we were driving into the city and not out to the lake. We pulled up to a rundown house just south of downtown Tampa. I was told to stay in the truck and wait. The guy I was with went in the house and left me in the truck for about fifteen minutes. I was a bit confused, but I knew where we were and what this guy was up to. When he returned he looked like a kid on Christmas morning, wide-eyed and jittery, wanting to open his present. Speeding away from the house I began to feel sick in the pit of my stomach. I knew this night was headed for disaster. He was focused on one thing and it was not the fishing trip.

We pulled into a church parking lot and he unwrapped his present. It was a little white rock. I had never seen anything like it. He put it in a glass tube and began to smoke it. It was crack. This was a new drug and this was the first time I had ever seen it. It smelled horrible and I became nauseous. The faint white smoke filled the cab of the truck, which made my eyes burn. It was at this point that I began to realize that we probably were not going to make it to the lake. I began to become very angry and resented that I ever got excited about this trip. It was becoming a pattern in my life that every time something looked good it was just a façade to something bad.

We sat in the parking lot for over an hour while this guy I barely knew got high. Finally we left to go fishing but the excitement had gone and now I just wanted to go home. I had no say and we were off lake bound and I was just along for the ride.

Once we reached the lake we launched the boat from the trailer, made any final adjustments and we were off. Once on the water I decided to give the trip a second chance. I figured that we were already here, why not have some fun? On our way out to the fishing spot this guy saw a new motor on a little boat that was tied up at one of the docks. We pulled up to the boat and examined it to see how easy it would be to steal the motor. Here we go again! Why could I just not have a normal fishing trip? Is that too much to ask?

We went back to the truck to get some tools and returned to the little boat. He worked on the boat for a while with no success. I don't know if he lacked mechanical knowledge or if he was just high, but he could not take the motor off the boat. Next thing I knew we were towing the little boat back to the truck. I knew what we were doing was wrong but I couldn't help but chuckle to myself when we pulled away from the dock with this little boat in the bed of the truck and our boat in tow. What were we doing? Was this guy so hard up for a high that we really needed that motor so bad? I would soon find out the answer to this question.

When we hit the shore I was in amazement as to what was going to happen next. Once we were situated and ready to go we put the little boat in the bed of the truck and put our boat back on the trailer. We sped away from the lake and pulled on to a side road where this guy could work on stealing the motor. Even at my young age I could see that what we were doing was only going to lead to trouble. By this time it had begun to rain and I went to sit in the truck. I couldn't help but think that this guy was an idiot. Sitting in the truck I was thinking how in the world I could be sitting here watching this fool struggle with this motor. Just as I was thinking that he called me to come help him.

Now I am standing in the rain on the side of the road helping to steal a motor off of a boat that we plucked out of the water just moments before. After some work, the motor was free and we dumped the boat on the side of the road. We drove to a pawnshop on the outskirts of Tampa and waited there for several hours till it opened. He sold the motor and we drove home. My night fishing trip turned into a night of drugs and theft. I never once put a line in the water.

A few days later there came a knock on the door. It was two police officers. They sat me down and asked if I knew why they were there. I told them the events of that night and they arrested the man that was going to take me fishing. This caused problems for us and we got kicked out of that house. We moved back to the country to live with Tammy's aunt and uncle. Then it was back to the same ole' lifestyle. The adults gone and me taking care of the girls like I always had.

HRS

Living in the country and not having much, if any, adult supervision, you can imagine that a kid's hygiene can get a bit lacking. This little fact would lead to the next adventure in my life. The younger of the two sisters began to form a rash in her diaper area. I did what I thought would help, but remember I was almost twelve years old and still had trouble taking care of myself much less a two year old with a rash that had begun to bleed.

I took the girl to a neighbor's house for help. Once there the neighbor helped me treat the rash. I would later learn that it was impetigo, which is a little more severe than a rash. The next day a large car pulled up to the house and a man and a woman stepped out and came to the door. They spoke with my father for a while and then I was called in the room. I could tell by the look on my father's face that what was about to happen was not going to go well for me. They sat me down on the couch and introduced themselves as agents for Health and Rehabilitation Services (HRS). This was the child protective agency in Florida. The neighbor had reported the rash and the current living conditions of us kids and this sparked an investigation. I was informed that the girls and I were going to be placed in foster care temporarily so that my father and Tammy could get back on their feet. I was to be placed in one home and the girls in another. This made me very upset because I had been taking care of them so long that I didn't want to be separated from them. I put up the best fight I could muster up, but it was to avail. I had no say in the matter and we were split up.

I went to my foster home and they went to theirs. In my first foster home I was placed with a family that had a daughter my age and two other foster children younger than me. This place was odd because when seven o'clock rolled around it was time to go to bed. The foster children were placed in one section of the house and a door was locked to separate us from them. There we would have to stay till they unlocked the door in the morning. This was almost as scary as being alone. I wouldn't say that they were mean people they just wanted to live their life and having foster kids running around made it a difficult task. I felt that I had to get out of this placement but was too scared to run. Besides, I was only going to be here for a couple of days. Well a couple of days had gone by and I was still in my placement. When I spoke to my caseworker she told me that I was going to stay longer until my father had his court date.

Even though it was pretty bad living with my father I did not want to be away from him. It was funny that I felt this way because when I got to the foster home I was a mess. I had lice and my skin was almost stained a dingy brown. I knew I was safe and could start to live a better life, but for some reason I did not want what was being offered to me. I was so confused and felt very lost. All I wanted to do was go home and be a normal kid. This began to make me angry and I began to act out. A couple of days turned into a couple of weeks.

I had my twelfth birthday in this foster home. I had a cake and one candle. They sang happy birthday and I blew out the candle. We ate cake and off to bed for the foster kids. My birthday lasted fifteen minutes. Don't get me wrong, I was grateful for the cake and party but I was tired of always getting the short end of the stick. Something had to change and I was no longer going to sit and let things happen.

I was very upset now that I had been in a placement so long and had not seen the girls. I demanded to speak to my caseworker and told her I wanted to see and be with the girls. She thought it would be a good idea as Tammy and my father had now married and by law the girls had become my stepsisters. A few days later I was reunited with my stepsisters and we were again together but not for long. The family the girls were with could no longer keep them for whatever reason and HRS was having trouble finding a placement that would house all three of us. I went to a home by myself and they went to another home with the understanding that we would be able to see each other a lot. As it turns out it was a good thing that the girls could not come with me. I wasn't sure if I had been placed in a foster home or a work camp.

I was the only foster kid in this home. They had two boys of their own that were younger than me and spoiled to the core. It was my job to wake up the boys and get them dressed, get them breakfast, and off to school. When we came home I had to do homework, which was hard because I had not been in school for almost two years (I was now twelve and in the fifth grade and struggling). Then I had a list of chores to have done by dinner. This included vacuuming the floors, cleaning the bathrooms and laundry. If this was done by dinner I could watch TV but I couldn't relax too long because I had to do dishes after dinner. I always wondered what the lady of the house did all day that made it so she was not able to help out.

Well, one day I was too sick to go to school and I found out. I was so mad when I saw what she did after we left for school. She went back to sleep. All day! After I saw this I was very defiant and argumentative. I didn't want to do anything. I was not a slave and I thought I had enough clout to stand up for myself. This led to a very rough stay at this placement. The more I resisted the workload the more I got. My anger got the best of me one day when I was mowing the lawn. Right in the middle of my mowing my foster dad came out and told me that one of the boys had spilled a pitcher of Kool-Aid in the kitchen and I needed to hurry and finish so I could clean it up. He said he was going to the store to pick up a few things and he wanted the job done by the time he came back.

I lost my mind and yelled, "I am not your god damn slave! You clean it up." This was not the best thing to do.

Without a second thought, I was thrown to the ground and instructed, "Have it cleaned up or your ass will be mine when I get back."

This only made me angrier and I tried to run from the back yard. As I ran next to my foster dad he grabbed me by the back of the collar and slung me back to the ground. Like a beaten down dog I went back to my chores and didn't put up much of a fight. My resolve had been pretty much destroyed by Tammy and my father. I had reached a point where the fight was not worth it. Just giving in seemed to be the best thing to do.

I made it through by talking to the girls and keeping the hope that my father would soon come for me. The one good thing this placement did for me was that I got to go to church and I met a kid that I got along with very well. His name was Frankie and we became good friends. He and his family knew I was a foster kid and they accepted me into their family with open arms. This was a good thing because I soon found out that my father had missed many court dates and I was now a ward of the state. Then I found out that the family I was with was going to move and I was going to be placed somewhere else.

I had gotten comfortable with the friends I had made and didn't want to lose them. I went to Frankie's parents and asked them to become foster parents and take the girls and me in. this was a huge task to ask someone to take on. They thought about it and agreed. After they were cleared to be foster parents the girls and I moved in. This was the first time in my life that I felt what it was like to have a family. We fit in quick with their family. We were going to school and eating good food. I was finally getting healthy and for the first time I saw the girls happy. I was finally able to be a kid and it felt great. I was out playing after school and riding the three-wheeler, I was doing things a kid my age should be doing. More than being a kid, I was finally protected from those that preyed on my sisters and me.

I was no longer a street kid and I could put a smile on my face knowing that I had nothing to fear. The foster family we were with taught me many valuable lessons. I was taught to respect myself and that I had value. I was able to go to church and made many new friends. There were times that I wished I was adopted by this family and I could live happily ever after.

I lived there for a while and started a new life and loved how it was going. I knew that my father had pretty much had given up on me and I guess in some way I moved on and was ok with it. I was sad that I never really had a real father to speak of. I would like to say that he did the best he could to raise me but I just don't feel he tried.

I turned thirteen in this home and was on my way to recovering from the past few years. Time came for me to move on and I was faced with a decision that no kid should have to make. My caseworker came to me and told me that my foster parents wanted to adopt me. I was excited, but that was not the choice I would have to make. That choice would come a few days later. The night before I was to be adopted a phone call from my caseworker. He gave me news that my brother, two sisters and other family were in Arizona looking for me. Now that they have tracked me down, they wanted me to come live with them. This was the choice that I had to make.

I loved my foster family and wanted to be with the girls. On the other hand I missed my brother and sisters and wanted to be with them. I couldn't have it both ways and I needed to choose what I wanted to do. This was a choice I couldn't make. I thought about it many different ways so that I would make the right choice. As hard as it was, I made my choice. I would leave the girls and go live with my family in Arizona.

Arizona

Before I knew it I was looking out the back window of a car watching my foster family and the girls fade out of sight. It was a sunny morning and I could feel the heat from the sun beat down on my face. I sat in the back seat of that car wondering if I had made the right choice. I thought about all the craziness and hardship that I had I lived through in the last few years and I began to feel at ease with my decision. I knew I would miss the girls but I knew they were in good hands. I had become their parent by default and I couldn't help but to think about their welfare. Driving down that long dirt road I began to breathe easier and my mind was put at ease. I could relax and be a kid.

I was driven to the airport in Tampa, Florida and boarded a plane with my caseworker to fly to Phoenix, Arizona. I was very excited and very sad at the same time.

When I landed, I could not contain myself. I knew that my sister Tammy was in the terminal waiting for me. My aunt Judy was there also and I was nervous to meet her. I know I had met her when my mother died but I did not remember. All I knew was the bad things that my father said about her. When I got off the plane I was greeted by my new family and I knew that I made the right choice. No matter how hard it was I did what was best for me.

The adjustment to my new family was not easy. We came from two different lifestyles. I was a street kid with a rough exterior. Now I lived in a house with five girls and one boy. They were members of the Church of Jesus Christ of Latter Day Saints and had never seen or experienced anything I have. This made it hard for me and it posed a great challenge for me. I was quickly introduced to the LDS church and soon began to take lessons to learn about it. I felt that it was something I wanted and knew was true. I soon got baptized.

Things happened real fast for me. I was bumped up a grade and now I was in the seventh grade and I quickly started sports. I was always a good athlete and this would prove to be one of my saving graces. I was an average student and really did not like to go to school but I loved sports and that kept me on an even playing field. I settled in with my new family and knew that was where I was going to spend the rest of my childhood. Eighth grade came and I was doing well. My sister was the coach of my softball team and we were city champs. This was awesome because it felt good to be back doing things with my sister.

We had a little reunion where all of us kids got together. It was the first time in seven years that all of us had been together. Life was on an upswing and I was doing well. I still had some contact with my father and Tammy but for the most part I was free from them.

We moved across town and I changed schools, which was good for me. The school I had just come from was overrun with gangs and drugs. This was the early nineties when gangs were wildly popular. There were plenty of days that I had to run from a mob of MVL gangsters because I looked in their direction. It was nice to leave that environment because I could feel myself slipping back into my old ways. I was a street kid and that is what I knew, so when I was given the opportunity to change I took it and ran. I was afraid to get in trouble and I saw myself headed that way again.

I was embraced at my new school because I had grown a lot in the time I was living in Arizona. At the age of fifteen I was six feet tall and weighed two hundred and fifty pounds. I had just moved into one of the best junior high schools for football in the city. This is how sports kind of saved me and kept me on track. I was very good at football and had the size to be a star. I did very well that year earning awards for the most outstanding lineman. Our team won the city title and set me on the road to success. This season thrust me into limelight in high school sports.

When I went to high school I continued to have much success playing football. I got to play varsity my junior and senior years. I even played some my sophomore year. When I was a junior we won the state championship in the 5A division, which is the highest level. I began to get letters from colleges who were interested in having me play football for them. I was right where I needed to be coming up to my senior year of football. I was part of a high school football team that was getting national attention and personally I was one of the top linemen in the state and western region. I was working out regularly and my body was beginning to form into something great. I was six foot three, weighing two hundred and seventy five pounds. I was very quick for my size and that would help me in my quest to become a college football player.

You should know by now that anytime things get really good for me something will throw a wrench into it. As I was getting ready for the upcoming season and football camp I met a girl that I quickly feel in love with. Her name was April and she was a freshman at Arizona State University (ASU). Even though I was older than her, I was still in high school in my senior year. One day I was sitting in the congregation of her church waiting to listen to a friend speak when she was called up to the stand to receive and medallion for her hard work. My friends and I sat there and made fun of her the whole time. She was kind of tall and had braces. This made for easy pickings when it came to making fun of her. It was some time before I was to see her again.

When I did see her again it was at a country church dance. We were both member of the Church of Jesus Christ of Latter

Day Saints. You might know it by the more familiar name... the Mormons. Saturday night dances were real popular in the eighteen and over crowd. On this particular night, April and two of her friends were huddled in a corner debating if I was fat or if I was muscle. At that time I was muscle. I was heading into my senior year of football and I was working out like a freak. Anyway, they were daring each other to dance with me and find out. April claims she was the loser but I still think she was the winner of the bet.

We danced for one song and hit it off great. Then we danced another. And another. We finished the night off and she gave me her number. I called her the next day. I know I should have waited the three day rule but I was leaving for football camp and really wanted to talk to her. I spent most of the next day and most of the night talking to her on the phone. We hit it off great and she was all I could think about. That week at football camp was the longest week of my life, not only was it physically tough it was mentally grueling. All I could think about was this girl I met and how much I wanted to talk to her and get to know her more. I should have only been focused on football but I couldn't get April out of my mind.

I know what you are thinking, but she had the braces off and she was enrolled in three different aerobics classes and she was looking good. At night I would close my eyes and try to remember what she looked like the night of the dance.

When I returned home from camp we began to see each other again. We were full speed right from the start. I was spending every spare moment with her and loving it. I don't know how I was able to keep that schedule. I must have been blinded by love. I would wake up, run before school started, go to school, and then practice. After practice I would then run again. I was part of a group known as the tons of fun club. These were the kids that were too heavy and needed to shed some pounds. Our football coach wanted players that were fast not big.

After my running I would go see April and stay out till one or two in the morning. I did this for a long time, keeping up this schedule day in and day out. Soon I was spending so much time with her that my football was beginning to suffer. I know if I had stayed more focused I would have had many opportunities come my way. I was fast becoming one of the top offensive linemen in the state. I was getting letters from many colleges but made an oral commitment to play at Oregon State University. Things were going good for me and I was finally feeling that my life was going to be headed down easy street. As I have stated before, when all seems right something goes wrong.

This was the case with April. We had become very involved and we were even talking about getting married after I had finished high school. The plan was simple to me: we would get married and move to Oregon. She could transfer up there and all would be well. Before I could propose the plan to her my life would change. As I said we were very involved. We were very sexually active and making some very poor and ill advised choices.

The night of Thanksgiving 1993, my family had traveled to Colorado for the holiday and I had to stay home because we were in the state playoffs and I needed to be here for the team. April told her mom that she was spending the night at a friend's house. Well, you might have guessed that she came to stay with me. We spent all night doing things that would change the course of our lives. I am convinced that this was the night that my oldest son was brought into my life.

It was soon after that I would find out April was pregnant. I would be lying if I said it was a surprise. This is the number one time in my life that I wished I had someone to lead me in the right direction. I was still in high school and was going to have a kid. I was as scared as I could be and not able to think like an adult. We had made plans to get married after I graduated high school so it was easy now for us to want to get married. We began to make plans and get things in order so that we could get married.

I think it was a few weeks into this whole process when we had a heart to heart talk and decided that getting married was probably not the best decision. It was more April than I wanting to separate and not get married. I remember that night very well. I left her house and ran away as fast as I could. I was so upset that I could not control my emotions. I began to cry as hard as I ever had before. I was so upset that I began to vomit. It had felt like my heart was ripped out. What was I going to do now? I had already called Oregon State University and told them I was not going to come. Now the woman I love who is carrying my baby, just told me that I would not be part of her life.

The next week was my version of hell on earth. I went from anger to relief, from sadness to being on top of the world. No matter how I felt I knew in my heart that I wanted to be with April. I guess it was a week or so when April and I began to talk about the fact that we were going to have a baby together and we needed to come to some kind of agreement on what we were going to do. We decided that it was important that we stay friends and work together to make the right decisions for our kid. To lay out the rules and what was expected we went to a place that we could play mini golf and talk it all out. Depending on whom you ask this was the best or worst thing to do. On the fourth hole there was a cave that you had to walk through to get to the next hole. Once inside the cave it was clear that we were going to be together. Without hesitation we began to kiss. This was it we had committed to each other that moment. The rest of that night we talked out our future together. We had decided that we wanted to be married and we should do it before she showed too much.

So there it was. I was a senior in high school with a pregnant girlfriend and no job. As I look back now, I think how crazy I was to think I could make it. I know now how hard it is to raise a family, but back then I was young and full of energy. This fact helped me through some pretty hard times. No matter what challenge was tossed in my path, I was going to overcome and be successful.

Spring break my senior year, while my friends were going to Mexico I was getting married. It was a small ceremony in the Mormon Church that we were attending. The Bishop of that church was a good friend to April and I. We had our family there and a few friends. There wasn't much money so the celebration was simple and quaint. We had our reception n the clubhouse of the apartments we were moving into. The flowers came from a funeral home. They were cheap and they were no longer needed. It was all set up and, much to my surprise, the wedding and reception all looked really beautiful. Once the reception started I quickly forgot where we were and under what circumstances we had all assembled.

We had a good support so we received a lot of money and gifts that would start us off right. Several of my friends rushed in and kidnapped my new bride and left a ransom note demanding that I raise a certain amount of money before they would bring her back. After much begging and pleading I raised the money necessary to get April back. Back at home after the reception I took a few minutes to count the money and prepare myself for the rest of my life. It was time to take care of the business of raising a family.

We took a small honeymoon in Prescott and we were officially married. When we came back we moved into our apartment and got back to school. I had a schedule that consisted of me going to school the first half of the day and working at a car dealership in the afternoon. I also worked on Saturdays so I could make forty hours each week. It was hard, no doubt, but I was excited and full of life with big goals so it was a good living to me. Soon my first son was born and I was filled with so much pride I was bursting at the seams. He was a spitting image of me and at the first moment I saw him I knew I must do whatever it takes to make sure that he would never see or do the things I did when I was a child. I felt as though I was entrusted to take this kid, and through him I could right all the wrongs that had happened to me and my siblings. This was the time for me to keep my promise to myself and make sure that nothing I went through would ever come close to my kids.

Dad, Husband, Provider

I was motivated to do right and be the best I could be. When you become a father it gives you such a sense of pride that you feel like you can conquer the world. Well, I felt that pride plus I had the doubts of many driving me to succeed. There were many people that would support me on the surface but doubt me when my back was turned. I knew they felt this way even though I never said anything. I took that doubt and turned it into something that motivated me to prove all them wrong. I never got mad at these people, because what they felt was justified. After all I was nineteen, married, and making five fifty an hour. To boot, I had just graduated high school and was a father. I know that from the outside it looked like I would fail.

It was that fear that made me do things that most nineteen-year-old kids never think about. April and I had agreed that I should go to college to so I could get the education that would help our little family. I needed to keep working, so I enrolled in the local community college so that I could go to school at night and still be able to work days. I had two desires in my life as far as a career goes. I wanted to be either a firefighter or a physical therapist. This particular college had a great fire science program, so that was my focus. I was never a good high school student, so when I got into college it was even harder because I had the freedom to chose if I wanted to go or not. My grades were not the best. I used everything as an excuse. If it wasn't my work schedule, it was that I didn't feel good, or that I could see April needed help with the baby so I should stay home and help. Needless to say, college in this environment was going to be difficult.

Quickly, life began to set in and it was beginning to bury me. It is fair to say that I was becoming angry at the fact it was hard and I was young. I was seeing friends out enjoying life and I was worried about bills and babies. I never really expressed this to anyone but my biggest regret in life was not going to college to play football. This ate at me as time passed because I slowly realized that I could have gone and had my family too. This was a hard pill to swallow. One day, I was driving past my old high school and I saw men practicing football. I knew it was not the school team because they were men and it was not the traditional football season. I saw these men for a week before I decided to stop and investigate what they were up to.

When I went out to the field I was greeted by a man that introduced himself as the owner of a semi-pro league that played in Phoenix. We talked in length about who I was and what my situation was. He went on to tell me that this was a league for people in similar situations as mine and he thought that I should give it a try. I was told that this was a new league and that they had just finished their first season and this was one of the all-star teams. I was also told that they had not had the turn out that they wanted and for twenty bucks I could play. Looking back, I laugh because I had never played a single down of football in this league, but I was on the all-star team.

They tossed another roadblock at me as soon as I paid my twenty bucks. They told me that the league does not pay or give you anything because it would void any college eligibility. This meant that I would have to get my own equipment. When I took this home to April she was livid and totally against me playing. I guess it was a way for me to recapture some of what I gave up. I was able to get equipment from several sources but I had to buy a helmet. The only one I could find and afford was a used one that had most of the padding missing. It did not have the forehead pad or the air bladder that provided the safety. I never practiced with the team I just showed up on game day and quickly went over some plays. They put me a starting right tackle and off I went.

After the game I was approached by four coaches and offered spots on their teams. I was new to the league and committed to a team. I would later change teams because I had met another lineman in this whole process and he got me to play for them. This was a good thing because we were the next year's State Champions. Our quarterback got a scholarship to play at the University of Central Arkansas and told them the only way he would go is if they gave me a scholarship as well. April hated that I played football and this led to much contention in our marriage. I was torn between being a family man and living my dream. I saw how I could play football and have a family. I learned from my past that I could do it. I was in turmoil over what to do. The deciding factor was the fact that this college was the number two physical therapy school in the country at that time.

You would think this would make it easy but it was the hardest decision I ever had to make. You see, April was eight months pregnant with our second son. She had never been away from her mom, and now I was asking her to move across the country. After much discussion, tears, and fights it was agreed that we would go. I flew out to Arkansas to accept the scholarship and find a place to live. My friend had already moved out there and was able to help me out. As I soon found out everyone was willing to help me out, I found a house on an alumni's property.

It was a funny house. It was a converted workshop that they turned into a three-bedroom house decorated in school colors. They were nice people that barely charged us rent and gave us full access to the property. I came back to Arizona to share the good news and pack up. By now April was eight and a half months pregnant and totally uprooting her life. I knew this was hard on her and struggled with that for a long time. I doubted if what I was doing was right. I couldn't help but feel it was right. I was going to a school to play football and get the education that would allow me to be a physical therapist. I thought that I would use football as an excuse to stay in and do well at school. After all that is what I did in high school.

It took four days, but we made the move to Arkansas and I began to practice while April was trying to adjust to her new life.

Our second son was soon born on the same day as our first son two years apart. With the arrival of our second son I thought it would make it easier on April. I thought that she would feel better and be able to get out and see the town. As it turned out it only made it harder. We were slowly falling into debt and it was beginning to put a lot of pressure on our marriage. Soon after giving birth, April got a job at the local Wal-Mart in the bakery. She would go to work at night after I got home and I would care for the kids. She was the doughnut maker working the graveyard shift. Her hours would cause her to sleep all day, and me and the boys were feeling the strain of that. I wanted nothing more than to make this college thing work, but the defining moment came when I was working out one fall morning.

I was squatting and I had some heavy weight on the bar. I was on number seven when I went down. I never came up. I had torn my patella tendon on my left knee. It was determined by the doctors that it was up to me if I wanted to have a surgery or not. I decided not to have the surgery and tried to rehab my knee. It is safe to say that when a college lineman gets hurt, he better be the best or he will be forgotten. I now use the term 'disposable commodity' to describe what a college lineman is. When I got hurt, all the free stuff and special treatment went away. Our money situation continued to get worse and the stress level was reaching a boiling point.

I was standing in the doorway of our bedroom one day, watching April sleep and listening to the baby cry when I decided that I needed to do what was best for my family. I made plans with my parents to move back home where I had help caring for my family. This was a hard time in my life because for a second time I was giving up my dream to ensure that I held strong to the promise I made to myself. I can't say I was mad because I would always do what is best for my family before I would think of myself, but I couldn't help but feel crushed. I had two opportunities to play college football and I never played one down. I remember driving away from the town crying out loud for what was happening to me at that moment. I have spent many years thinking, "what if?"

Home Sweet Home

When we returned home we moved in with April's mom. We were trying to get our finances back in control. Soon we moved out and it was back to everyday life for a young married man with kids. I continued to play and coach in the semi-pro league for several more years. I was working and we seemed to be regaining steam when we found out that our third boy was on the way. I couldn't believe it! I was enjoying being a father of boys and my life was very rewarding. I was involved in youth sports, still playing football and working. Things were going great when I learned how blessed I was.

It was shortly after our fourth son was born that I would learn how fragile life is and not to take for granted the little ones in our life.

It was a routine night for our family. We had eaten dinner and the three boys and I were watching TV down stairs. April and our third son were upstairs at the computer. Our son had been feeling sick and running a fever all day. He wanted to be comforted by his mom so she took him with her and I was to take the other boys and give them some quiet time. I remember I was sitting on the couch when I heard the most blood-curdling scream I have ever heard. It was April screaming that our son had fallen on scissors, or at least that is what I thought she said.

When I got up stairs I saw my son flopping around like a fish out of water. I then knew she was yelling seizure and began to panic. I had just completed training to be an EMT (emergency medical technician) but when it is your son it seems to cloud your thinking. I had April call 911 while I took him to the front door to wait for the paramedics. While at the front door, his breathing began to slow to a stop. This made my blood run cold with fear. I was frozen and not responding to what was going on. It was as if my mind had shut down and I was unable to apply anything I had learned. I could hear the sirens but we lived pretty far out and the fire service had not been established that far out yet. I knew it was up to me to help my son if he had any chance of survival.

I gave him two rescue breaths and checked his pulse. While checking his pulse he began to breathe again. I began to feel my mind come back to life and began to feel I had things under control.

This did not last long before he stopped breathing again. I repeated the process again with similar results. I was growing increasingly anxious and scared. Why was it taking so long for the paramedics to show up? The sounds of the sirens were still in the background but they seemed to not get any closer.

A third time he stopped breathing. This time I could not get him to breathe. I ran through the same sequence of events that had worked before but it was not working. At this point I truly felt that this might be the last time I see my son alive again. Why was this happening and why did he not breathe? I was out of options and still no paramedics.

It was at that moment that I leaned down and whispered, "I love you buddy and need you to stay. If you need to go home I understand but I need you here. I love you."

I got the feeling that I should hit him on the chest and that is exactly what I did. With all the power I could muster up I hit him square on the chest. I guess it jolted him because he took a big gasp and began to breathe once more. In an instant I went from being terrified to being completely elated. My body was shaking from fear and excitement.

The paramedics showed up and began working on him. They packaged him and rushed him and April to the hospital. Our neighbors came to take care of the other boys while I went to meet up with them at the hospital. As I was driving, it hit me that my son might be gone when I get to the hospital. I began to cry uncontrollably at the thought of losing one of my sons. What would I do if I lost that part of my life?

When I got to the hospital I walked into his room expecting the worst. When I pushed back the curtain he was sitting up in his bed drinking water. At that moment I was filled with a joy I had never felt before. It is true what they say about not knowing what you have till you lose it. That night I thought I was going to lose a son and it shook me to the core.

He had a febrile seizure. It is caused by your temperature being too high. It is pretty common with young kids and should last thirty to forty five seconds. His lasted over five minutes! When I said goodbye to my son that night I accepted that he might die. I truly knew what it meant to be a father. I knew what it means to make the tough choices in your kid's life. The knowledge that we can't control life was never more evident than that night. I also know what happened that night was no accident. He has a purpose on this earth. As it turns out, he suffered no long lasting effects from this.

Life got back to normal and we were on our way to creating a good solid life that went against everything that was supposed to happen. April graduated college and I was working my way up the career ladder. Things were going great for us at this time in our life. I felt as though I had arrived and nothing could go wrong now. We bought our first house and were in the process of starting a party rental business. Like I said, things were looking up.

We had settled into a great life typical of the American dream. April had started to work as a kindergarten teacher at the neighborhood school. The boys were doing great and I continued doing well in my work and starting my new business. In an instant thing changed and this set off a series of events that could not be fixed.

The Beginning Of The End

I was at my work delivering bottled water when I was hurt in an accident. I was getting a bottle off the truck when it got caught and flipped over my wrist. It was my instinct to hold on the bottle to keep it from smashing on the ground. My efforts were in vain. Before the bottle hit the ground it snapped my wrist and in that moment my life would yet again be changed. The doctor came to the conclusion that I needed surgery to repair a damaged cartilage.

After I had that surgery I was not allowed to return to work for some time. Anyone who has been hurt at work knows that you don't get paid as much as you do when you are at work, so the bills began to pile up. I was cleared to work and I thought things would get back to normal. We started to get back on track and life was less stressful. I was working and the business was starting to take off and make some real money.

Then came the day that my wrist began to lock up and hurt very bad. I went for a checkup and x-rays revealed that the bones in my hand were rubbing together and had begun to separate. I was in a lot of pain and needed relief. This required me to have another surgery that would put six-inch long pins through my wrist to try to hold the bones together. The pins would stay for ten weeks. Because I worked with my hands, this again would cause me to miss more work. By this time, the financial situation was getting bad for us and our relationship was feeling the effects. We were fighting a lot and April was going to have to take a full time position as a teacher.

It got real hard for April to see me sitting around the house while our financial situation got worse. We were falling apart fast and I began to feel sorry for myself, which in return put more stress on our relationship. After the ten weeks had passed, the pins were removed and I was again allowed to go back to work. By this time the damage was done and our relationship was on the rocks. We were no longer in love and we were staying together to save our boys. This was the beginning of the end for us.

After returning to work I thought things at home would get better but they continued to decline. Our communication was lacking and we could no longer function. There were times we would sit in silence for hours not even acknowledging the fact that we were in the same room. I think this was the first time that I had begun to accept the fact that my marriage was starting to crumble. I remember sitting on the bed after a very heated fight, lost in thought. A tear rolled down my cheek as the magnitude of my situation sank in. we were far apart now and the distance between us was too great to patch up.

Knowing that I was in a failing marriage, I began to ponder and question if I was a good father and if I kept my promise I made to myself so many years ago. Had I done enough to make sure I was nothing like my father, or was I headed down the same path? Divorce was a huge black eye to me and I was determined to fix the situation. I wanted so much to prove all those that doubted me wrong.

I started to make a list of things I needed to do and began to make a plan. There was one common factor that kept popping up. I somehow felt that I had unresolved issues with my father. It kept drawing me back to my childhood and I couldn't get over some of the things that he did. In my adult eyes he was an evil person who had gotten away with too many wrong doings. He was free and doing as he pleased and somehow this had an adverse effect on me.

When I got honest with myself I realized that I had become what I told myself I would never become and that is someone who blames their present on their past. My mind was focused on finding the answers in hopes that it would give me closure on my past and help me to better my present. It needed to happen quickly. April and I were falling apart quick and I had no idea how to stop it. I was lost and there was no one looking for me. I was on my own and not sure where to go. A simple twist of fate would soon point me in the right direction.

Bye Bye Birdie

Miles away and far removed from my father, I had become comfortable in the fact that I had not seen or spoke to him in many years. Even though I was that far removed, my father's choices would one more time affect my life. He was living in Ohio working as an over the road truck driver and living with his wife, Tammy. I received a call one night that my father was being indicted on charges of three counts of gross sexual imposition on a minor. In short, he was molesting children as he had done many years ago to my sister. I instantly grew angry at what was going on, but I decided to let the system take care of it. I would receive updates as time went on and it began to sound as though he might get a pass and get off.

This was it! If he got locked up and went away, I could get that closure I was looking for. This could change my life and get me back on the right track. I know it is hard to understand, but it's kind of like riding a bike with a flat tire; you can make it move, but is it really going to get you anywhere? I need to face the beast. Eye to eye and man to man. If I was ever to truly get over my past I had to face this demon and lock it away.

Lying in bed one night, I told April I needed to go to Ohio and make sure he went away for his actions. It was instant and April supported me going. She knew I had my demons and she too wanted me to deal with them.

Within a week I was on a plane headed to Ohio. I was excited and scared at the same time. I wasn't sure what I was going to do when I got there but I could not let him get off without a challenge. Once I landed, I was greeted by my brother who I had not seen in about six years and we were en route to his house. My brother began by telling me that my father had caught wind of his possible arrest and tried to flee town. The lead detective intercepted him at a storage facility and explained that if he was going to leave he would be arrested. This caused my father to move into a motel and wait for the outcome of his case.

Same story as I had when I was a kid. Living in a motel and on the run. I would like to say I was shocked but in some way I had grown to expect things like this. We drove through the old town I had lived in so long ago and a rush of memories came flooding back. We drove by my old baseball field where I had played Little League and by my Elementary school. I was overrun with emotions as we reminisced about the times when I was young. My excitement hit a peak when we pulled on to the street where my grandmother had lived and where I had grown up. It had been many years since I left but it seemed like nothing had changed. I was somehow in a time warp. That old garage where I rescued my sister, the alley where I was the entertainment for my brother and his friends and the house where we lived with grandmother. It was all there and it felt like a long weekend had passed and I had returned back to that time when I was young.

The next morning was all business. With the help of my sister in law, Missy, we began to lay out our plan of attack. Missy is very vocal and the descriptions of what was going on got me fired up, and I was determined to do whatever it took to put my father behind bars. I was told that the lead detective was not too helpful and he wasn't giving many answers to the questions Missy was asking. I knew this would be the first thing I needed to do. I had to speak to the detective and find out the status of the case.

When we arrived at the police station I waited to speak to the detective for about thirty minutes. My palms were sweaty and my heart was beating out of control. Had I made a mistake? Was I able to do this? These were all questions that began to pop up in my head. I began to doubt myself and wanted to get back on the plane and leave. In my mind I had made a mistake by going to Ohio and it was going to blow up on me. I actually reached out to grab Missy by the arm and tell her, "let's just forget it and go," when I heard my name called. I spun around to see the detective standing in the doorway, waiting for my response. This was it. There was no turning back. I had to do what I came to do.

We were led to an interview room where I was placed at the end of a long table. I sat down along with Missy and waited for instruction. When the detective asked, "how can I help you?" I froze. I did not know what to say. I had this big speech planned out and a list of demands. That all seemed to fly out the window when I was put on the spot. Missy saved me and began by introducing me to the detective and asking if he had any info. Once she did this I instantly became relaxed and my thoughts began to fall in place.

I wanted to know why it had taken so long to formally press charges on my father and how could he still be free to work and possibly do this to other kids. I wanted to know why they just let him continue his life for almost one year and not arrest him and charge him. In my head it seemed simple and I was frustrated that nothing was being done. It was explained to me that it took time to make sure that nothing was overlooked and that when they went to arrest him they would have all their ducks in a row. I stressed to the police that I was only in town for a short time and I wanted to see him put away so no one else would get hurt. Of course the judicial system does not work on my schedule and I could tell that the detective was getting a little annoyed with me. I pulled a letter out of my pocket that I had from another victim that was too afraid to come forward to say something. It was a letter that described the events and actions perpetrated on her when she was young. Because of the time that had passed, more charges could not be filed but that letter would come into good use later in my trip. I was instructed to go home and wait for the system to run its course. I think the detective could see the desperation on my face when he paused mid sentence and said, "unless." When he said that I knew I would achieve my goal.

"Unless you can catch or prove he is doing something to break the law."

There it was. My mission for the next few days.

My father was due back from one of his trips in his truck and we needed to prove that he was part of something illegal. We knew that Tammy was dealing crack out of the motel and there was a rumor that there was an assault rifle in the room as well. Being a convicted felon, either one of these things would cause them to arrest him and hold him till the charges came down for the sexual activity. We began our investigation by talking to people that knew what was going on in the motel room. We soon knew for sure that they were dealing drugs and in fact they had an assault rifle too. Now it was time to wait.

My father was due home the next day and we would try to put him in the same location with Tammy and the drugs. The following day Missy had received a phone call that it was getting out among some church members that we were trying to get my father arrested and they were upset wondering how we could be so cruel and tell so many lies. My father was attending the same church as Missy and he had become very popular amongst the congregation and they actually had taken his side. I wanted to keep a low profile and did not want to tip off my father that I was there. I asked Missy to arrange a meeting with the pastor of the church where I could talk to him to explain what was going on. This is where the letter I had would become so important.

I sat in front of the pastor and told him my story and the story of my older sister. I told him of the things I had been through and how my father had turned his back on me while I was in foster care. Then I gave him the letter and asked him to read it. The room was silent and you could feel the emotion as the pastor read the letter. When he finished, we sat in silence for what seemed like several minutes. With his head hung down the pastor said, "I had no idea."

With that, my story was validated and we acquired a new ally. There was a troubled look on the face of the pastor that prompted me to inquire. He stated that he was troubled by the fact that my father had used his truck to entertain kids and women at church functions and the fact that he was an over the road truck driver gave him cause to wonder if this had happened to others. The realization that he might be right almost sent me to my knees. I sat there for a minute or two and then it dawned on me that I had two family members in county lock up right now that had close contact with my father and his truck when they were minors.

Later that day, after circulating the letter around to the church members and telling the story many times, I knew we needed to go to the county jail and ask the question to the two who were locked up. I guess it scared me a little because I did not do this for a couple of more days. We continued to play amateur detectives and try to link my father to illegal activity. This proved harder that I thought it was going to be. We could never get him in the motel at the right time, or we could never get concrete proof of what was going on. My father had no clue I was in town and I was in a rental car so on the last night of us playing detective we decided to drive right up to the motel and park a few spots down from the room and watch.

Just as we had thought, a car pulled up and backed into the space in front of the motel room of my father and Tammy. Two men get out and open the trunk. One of the men takes out a large shoebox and enters the room. A few minutes later he leaves counting money as he enters his car and drives off. We have it! The proof we needed that they were running drugs, but we still could not prove it to the detective. Feeling dejected and defeated, we left not sure what to do. My time had grown short and I would have to leave soon. I began to feel like I failed. I went to sleep that night giving up on the mission I had set out on.

I was awakened by Missy telling me that the pastor had just called, and that my father was arrested around four in the morning. We did it! We stopped my father from hurting anyone again. I was too excited to contain myself but I knew there was one more thing I needed to do. I needed to ask the two family members to see if they had been victimized by my father. I wanted so much for the answer to be no, but I knew in the pit of my stomach that would not be the case. I confronted the two and they both admitted they were sexually molested by my father. This sent shock waves of anger through my body. I was trembling and wanted to lash out and punch something. When I composed myself I asked to speak to the sergeant on duty and explained what happened and asked for it to be documented. I was given the assurance it would be done and I was excused to leave.

I sat down in the waiting room and tried to calm myself. The longer I sat there, the angrier I became. It was gone; there was no more fear. I wanted to confront my father and I had that opportunity if I wanted it. He was in one of the units in County lock up and all I had to do was ask.

My father had no clue I was in town and would never believe it was me that played a part in having him arrested. I knew I had to see him. I was filled with rage and I knew I would get justification for all the wrong he had done if I could just talk to him and let him know I knew all his misdeeds and evil doings. Even at this point as a grown man thirty years old he thought of me as his little buddy. I truly feel he thought I would feel the same. I asked to see him and sat in front of a television screen and waited. I wish I could have had a face-to-face meeting but the jail would not allow it.

I could tell by the look on his face that I was the last person he expected to be sitting on the other end.

"Bud, what are you doing here?" he asked.

I felt the blood run from my head and a tingle run down my spine. I wanted to kill him. I wanted to know what it would feel like to have him take his last breath as I applied pressure to his throat. My knuckles began to turn white and felt myself begin to lose control. I was better than he was and I wanted him to know it.

"Did you molest Laurie?" I asked.

I could see at that moment that his life came crashing down on him. I wanted him to be honest so I could somehow forgive him on that fact alone.

"What are you talking about?" was his reply.

"I want you to tell me what you did to Laurie."

I knew he was going to lie and try to play it off like he did when I was a kid.

"I did my time for that," he said, now a little annoyed at me.

"My question was, did you molest Laurie?" My rage hit an all time high.

"That's what that fucking Bishop and your Aunt said I did."

I couldn't take it any longer. I was angry with him for what he did in the past and the present. I wanted nothing more to do with him. I felt the blood pressurize up in my eyes as I prepared for what I was going to say next.

"I came here a week ago," I said. "I saw what you and Tammy are into and I what you have done in your life. I came here to put you away and make sure you don't hurt anyone else."

He began to speak but I cut him off.

"Shut up," I said. "You can't talk to me anymore. You stole my innocence and you did it to my family." He turned his head and closed his eyes.

This let me know he was hearing what I was saying.

"I want you to know that you left me unprotected, and I was molested by Tammy. But it didn't ruin my life. Neither of you could do that."

With that statement, his head snapped forward and I knew I had delivered the deathblow. I know what I said about Tammy crushed him, and at that moment I think he knew what it felt like to be one of us as a kid. Helpless.

"I know who and what you are," I continued. "I hope you never see the light of day again".

With that I slammed the phone down, breaking our connection and ending the conversation. I did not want him to speak and try to make excuses. I paused for a second and watched the screen go black. It was at that moment that I knew I would never see my father again, and oddly enough I was at peace with that.

I returned home with a new vigor and excitement for life. I felt like I had just closed a huge chapter in my life and I wanted to carry over to what I was dealing with at home. Subsequently, my father was convicted of the crimes he committed but was only given three years in Hocking Correctional Facility in Ohio. I had to take some satisfaction in this. I knew it would keep him off the streets and would label him as a sexual predator. This was not available the first time. I now knew I could move on with my life and begin rebuilding the damage that had been done. I was cleared to go back to work from my second wrist operation and I was motivated to succeed. I was going to make it right with April.

It's Final

Soon after returning to work, I reached up to answer the phone and it felt as though my wrist fell apart. With a clunk, I felt one of the worst pains I have ever felt. I was done. My wrist no longer worked and I was in severe pain. I returned to the doctor and learned that there was nothing to do but fuse my wrist. This meant that I was going to be out of work for a long time, and again my family was going to suffer. I think it was this that really put the nail in the coffin for April. The stress and hardship became too much. She was not the only one that was pushed over the edge. I had begun to fall into depression caused by the pain and the feeling of being a failure. The surgery was to be approved by workers comp and they were in no hurry to approve a thirty thousand dollar surgery. In all it took six months from the time I got hurt the final time till they fused my wrist.

I could not deal with the pain any more. I gave up on all the pain medications I was taking. I was up to ten OxyContin a day. I had become a zombie and was not functional at all. I was losing my relationship with my kids and I did nothing to change. I had given up on all the things I loved most.

The pain was too great and my depression got deeper and deeper. I went one stretch where I did not sleep for thirteen days. I mean I lay down but it was impossible to sleep. I decided that it was time to get rid of the pain. I began to drink very heavily as a way to cope with the pain. It was common for me to go to the bar and drink a bottle of Jack Daniels. If I were tired I would just kill that bottle at home in fifteen to twenty minutes. Soon, this became the only way for me to get sleep. I had a routine of sitting all day feeling sorry for myself and dealing with severe pain. Then at night I would drink till I passed out. I did this for months.

April and I fell further and further apart. The pain was so bad that I fell so deep into depression that I was past the point of no return. I didn't care about anything or anyone. It was all about me and my family was paying the price.

It came time for me to have my surgery and I began to get excited. The thought of not having the pain and being fixed lifted my spirits. It was the afternoon before my surgery when I got a phone call at four thirty in the afternoon. It was the doctor's office. They had just received a phone call that the surgery was not approved. I was devastated. I lost my mind. It was as though my mind went blank and I sank so deep into depression that I was unable to think clearly. I went up stairs to my bedroom and locked my door. It was quiet, and things seemed to slow down. I reached under the bed and grabbed the plastic black case. I placed it on the bed and opened it up. There it was, my .40 caliber Ruger pistol. I had made up my mind that I was going to put a bullet through my wrist.

In my depressed state I felt that there was no other way to get my wrist fixed. I slid the clip into the gun and slowly cocked it. By now my face was wet with tears. As my breathing got deeper and deeper, my pulse raced. I held the gun tight to my wrist and gripped the gun with my sweaty hand. I was caught in an argument with myself. I was ready to do it but at the same time I trying to talk myself out of it. I was ready, and prepared my mind to do it. I could feel the trigger move as I began to squeeze.

Right at that moment I heard my oldest son calling my name. He was walking upstairs to find me so he could ask for a Capri Sun. It was if I had snapped back to reality and I began to cry uncontrollably. I couldn't believe what I was doing. I had reached a point where I was willing to do anything to relieve my pain. I sat there on the edge of my bed shaking and staring at my wrist in disbelief. How could I have let it get this far and why did I not get help? I don't know the answer to that but I do know I needed someone to step up and help but it just was not there.

The next few months were blurry because I was drunk most of the time. Drinking would be the demise and the eye opener I needed. It was the night before Thanksgiving and April and I were out drinking at a party for a friend's wedding. The party went to the local bar where April and I both got very drunk. We began to fight and it got to be too much. We left and went home where there the fighting continued. It got out of hand and I pushed her. That kind of ended the fight but I took her cell phone and would not give it back. She wanted to call someone to come get her and I would not give her the phone back. She got very angry and threatened to call 911. In my drunken stupor I told her to call. She grabbed the house phone and dialed 911. When they answered, she panicked and hung up the phone. Of course they are going to call back. When they did she began to tell a story that was so far from the truth it is almost comical at this point. She went on to tell them that I was this huge man that was throwing her around. She went on to tell them that I had guns and she feared for her life. The truth was that I was almost passed out and really no threat at all.

While she was talking to them I got up and put on my pants, handed her the phone and walked down stairs. I grabbed a bottle of water and my ID. I walked out to my truck, dropped the tailgate and waited. In a few minutes there were police all over and I was taken into custody. As hard as it might be to believe what I am going to say is the truth. When I went to jail, it was like reality slapping me in the face. At once it seemed like the depression was gone and I somehow had clear thoughts of what I needed to do with my life and my marriage.

I sat there in the holding cell of the Sheriff's office looking at the man asleep on the floor wondering what crime he had committed. The hours had begun to pass by and the night had turned into day. I was in the holding cell just hoping that April would soon walk through the door and I could go home.

Hour after hour I was tormented with the thought that I would soon be out. After all I had done in my life I never once was incarcerated and I started to grow very impatient. Anxiety slowly engulfed my being and I knew I was in for a wild ride. I continued to sit on that bench in the cell and think about all the things I had done wrong, and I wished so much I could have changed them. I wanted to go home and make it right with April. Even though our lives had crumbled down around us and the outcome looked bleak, she was my best friend and we had four beautiful sons together. We had been married for almost thirteen years and that is hard to forget. By now there were many more people sharing the cell with me and the chatter among everyone was the fact it was Thanksgiving and how we all wanted to be home with our families.

I hung my head and tears began to well up in my eyes as I thought about my sons and the fact that this was the first holiday in their lives that I was not with them. Then the embarrassment of the reason why I was in jail added even more regret. How was I going to tell my sons what I had done? I let myself down by not upholding the level of respect I demanded out of them. How then could I expect it from them? With this one action, all my hard work was disappearing like it was never there. I felt like I failed my sons and that I could never look any one of them in the eyes again. That whole day I sat thinking of how they must have felt and what an uncomfortable position I put April in. She was left to cover for me while I sat in jail for my actions. This was the turning point in my life. I spent three days in that jail to think about what I had done and how I could make amends with what I had done.

I know three days may not sound like much but I had never been in jail before so it might as well have been three years.

When I was released, I knew what I needed to do. I was going to make things right with April and our sons. I was going to stop drinking and focus on my family. I was a new man; fired up and ready to go. I wanted to look my sons in the eyes and tell them the truth and man up for my actions. I wanted my life back and nothing was going to stop me.

I feel this is the point that our marriage really fell apart. April was done dealing with the financial hardship and I felt alone. We got to a point where we didn't really talk to each other at all. We had become strangers in our own house. We both were drinking hard and pretending that there was nothing wrong. I can still remember the very day that I knew April was done with me and our marriage. I could see that there was no more love in her eyes.

She simply looked at me and said, "I am done."

That was the afternoon after I was released from jail. I was escorted by a police officer to my house because there was an order of protection placed on me. With that, it was done. In the next couple of weeks April moved out and I was left alone in our house. The boy's rooms were empty and all the nice furnishings gone. I had sold most of my personal effect to help April and the boys get into a new house. I had tricked myself into believing that after some time we would patch things up and I would go live with them in the new house. This would not happen and we began our lives apart.

Oddly enough, I am not mad that I went to jail that night. It changed my life and I credit it for putting me back on the right track. I am not saying that I was perfect after that but I had a clear understanding of what I did not want as a father, husband or brother.

I am going to stop the story at this point. There are things that we all do that we are not proud of, and after all the things I have seen and done this is by far the time in my life I am least proud of. There has not been enough time passed for me to fully deal with my choices and actions. Sometimes, when all seems lost, I tend to do the extreme hoping that will be right the course. In my case it opened a crack in my life that could not be repaired.

I know now more than ever that the things we do and say have a ripple effect in others lives. I will tell you that after thirteen years of marriage, April and I have divorced. We share time with the boys and I think we have a good relationship even though we are divorced. Our sons are healthy and relatively happy. I am moving on with my life and trying to work hard at learning from my mistakes. I have a wonderful job working at a school with troubled youth who are in need of the kind of life experience I have. I now coach football in the hopes that someday when a young man comes to me and needs to my advice on what to do, I will be there for him. That is what I call a true paycheck. Working at this school has taught me that there are millions of stories like mine. I must admit that it saddens me to know that there are so many people that refuse to take care of their responsibilities and neglect the basic commitment that was made when they decided to have children. I guess it is easy for me to say this because I have made the decision to work my way out of that kind of life.

I know that not everyone will do the same things as I have but I don't understand why people accept what the world throws at them. Working with the youth has taught me that I am special and have a lot to give back. I know every day I make a difference and that helps to ease the pain of the past. I continue to deal with the past and have found that the more I share this story, the more I am able to accept what I have been through. I have tried to share this with my sister Tammy in the hopes that it would inspire her to write her story. I have heard bits and pieces of her story and it is amazing. What she has seen and done far outweighs what I have.

If I could get her to share it, it would change my life. I would like to take the time to say thank you to my sister Tammy and let her know that she has been my life and my strength. No matter the situation or what kind of trouble I seem to find, you are there waiting to stretch out your hand and save me. This is also true for my brother Doug. I want you guys to know that I know the sacrifice that was given in order for me to have a better live than you had it. I hope I can somehow repay you for all the love and sacrifice you gave. I know it was not easy and you gave up a lot. Again, I say thank you.

Sometimes I sit and wonder if I have lived my life the way it was supposed to be lived. To tell you the truth, I am not sure. Some days seem to drag on and cause me to question whether or not I did what was required of me. I know I have tried, but is that enough? I can say without a doubt that I did what I felt in my heart was right. I can only hope that I continue to be that example that my sons need to become great husbands and fathers. It has always been my goal to never be like my father and I know I succeeded in that endeavor. I know now more than ever that it doesn't matter where you have been or what you have done that matters but what you're doing and where you're going that counts.

Bobby Howell currently resides in Arizona, where he works at a group home for At Risk Youth. Every day he helps kids struggle through some of the same issues that he had to face alone.

email: **bobbyhowellstory@yahoo.com**

A special thank you

I need to take the time to say a special thank you to my friend, editor, and guide. While writing this book I faced many obstacles and roadblocks. Casey Grant took an interest in my book and stepped up to help lead me in the right direction. I was truly lost and needed help and you did that for me and I thank you for that. You have a special talent and you will be blessed for sharing it with me.

-Bobby

www.ingramcontent.com/pod-product-compliance
Lightning Source LLC
La Vergne TN
LVHW051133080426
835510LV00018B/2393